SCIENTIFIC
AMERICAN *SOURCEBOOKS*

ENDANGERED BIRDS OF NORTH AMERICA

APRIL PULLEY SAYRE

T F
C B
Twenty-First Century Books
Brookfield, Connecticut

Twenty-First Century Books
A Division of The Millbrook Press
2 Old New Milford Road
Brookfield, CT 06804

The maps featured in this book were created by Jeffrey L. Ward.

Library of Congress Cataloging-in-Publication Data
Sayre, April Pulley / Endangered birds of North America / April Pulley Sayre.
p. cm. (Scientific American sourcebooks). Includes bibliographical references and index.
Summary: Discusses why certain bird species are endangered and examines such examples as the
snail kite, piping plover, and whooping crane.
1. Birds—North America—Juvenile literature. 2. Birds, Protection of—North America—Juvenile
literature. 3. Endangered species—North America—Juvenile literature. [1. Birds—Protection.
2. Rare animals. 3. Endangered species.] I. Title. II.Series.
QL696.57.N7S39 1997   333.95'822'097—dc21   97-12793

ISBN 0-8050-4549-X

Printed in the United States of America
10 9 8 7 6 5 4 3

For Naturalist Tim Cordell of Potato Creek State Park in Indiana; and for all the other government employees whose committment, hard work, and quiet excellence make conservation programs succeed.

ACKNOWLEDGMENTS

Our thanks to the following people who reviewed portions of the manuscript and answered research questions: Paul R. Schmidt of the U.S. Fish and Wildlife Service; Dr. Jerome A. Jackson, professor of Biological Sciences, Mississippi State University; Dr. Paul W. Sykes Jr., Wildlife Research Biologist at the Patuxent Wildlife Research Center; Robert Pace, U.S. Fish and Wildlife Service South Florida Ecosystem Office; Scott Swengel, assistant curator of birds, International Crane Foundation; the staff of the U.S. Fish and Wildlife Service California Condor Recovery Program; and the staff of the National Fish and Wildlife Foundation, coordinators of Partners in Flight.

CONTENTS

Why Are Birds in Trouble?

*T*wo hundred years ago, passenger pigeons were so common in North America that flocks of them darkened the sky. One flock could contain millions of these birds. Single flocks stretched four miles wide and three hundred miles long! Yet today, passenger pigeons are extinct. The last one died in the Cincinnati Zoo in 1914.

No one can bring back the passenger pigeons. But people are working to prevent the extinction of other birds. The first step in this process is to identify what birds are endangered (what birds are in danger of becoming extinct). Endangered birds, such as the whooping crane, Bachman's warbler, and the wood stork, exist only in small numbers. They occupy only a small portion of their former range, the area they once inhabited. A bird, such as the northern spotted owl, is considered threatened if its population faces serious problems that are likely to make it become endangered sometime in the future. The United States Fish and Wildlife Service maintains a list of threatened species and endangered species in the United States. They also keep a list of some threatened and endangered species in the rest of the world.

Before a bird, or any other organism, is put on the list, scientists study it thoroughly. They need to estimate how many are left in the population. They need to find out what problems threaten the species. (A species is a group of organisms that can interbreed and produce young that are able to breed. The members of a species also have many characteristics in common.) Becoming "listed" is a process that can take many years. Currently seventy-four bird species are listed as endangered in the United States. Sixteen bird species are considered threatened. Ten other species are being considered for listing, but applications on their behalf have not been processed yet.

In the United States, the Endangered Species Act, passed in 1973, protects threatened and endangered species. Threatened and endangered species cannot be hunted, harassed, collected, bought, sold, imported, or exported without a special permit. Special permits are also needed to keep these species in zoos or to exhibit them.

Later revisions of the Endangered Species Act gave the United States government the responsibility to help an endangered population recover, as well. Soon after a species is listed as threatened or endangered, the United States Fish and Wildlife Service must come up with a plan to help the species increase in number. Many citizens and nonprofit groups also work to help endangered species, including endangered birds.

WHAT IS A BIRD?   From soaring eagles, to swimming penguins, to flitting warblers, to wading egrets; birds worldwide vary drastically in their shapes, sizes, and behaviors. Yet it is relatively easy to recognize a bird as a bird, whether it's a 250-pound (114-kilogram) ostrich or a 0.07-ounce

(2-gram) hummingbird. Birds have something no other animal does: feathers. These feathers keep birds warm and help them fly.

Birds, as a group, belong to the scientific class Aves. Like other vertebrates such as mammals and reptiles, birds have backbones. In addition to feathers, birds have bills, a distinctive feature. (The only nonbird with anything similar to a bill is the duck-billed platypus, a mammal.) Most birds fly, although ostriches, cassowaries, penguins, and some species of grebes, pigeons, parrots, rails, and other bird classifications do not. Nevertheless, the bodies of birds, in general, are adapted for flight. For example, they have hollow bones, which are very light. Their wings are powered by large, strong muscles attached to their keels—bony ridges in the middle of their chests.

Some birds have complex social lives. Many birds establish territories—areas that they defend from intruders. (Often territories are around nests or important feeding spots.) Many birds sing and carry out elaborate dances, dives, and feather displays, to both declare their territories and to attract mates. Birds lay hard-shelled eggs. Nests vary from a spot a killdeer clears on the ground to a hummingbird's complex woven nest of bark, animal fur, and spiderwebs. Birds, in general, invest a lot of energy in raising their young, compared with other animals whose young hatch from eggs. Bird parents must take care of their young for a relatively long time, although not as long as many mammals.

Ornithologists, scientists who study birds, believe that birds evolved from reptiles. The scales on birds' feet are similar to reptiles' scales. During the age of dinosaurs, 150 million years ago, a creature called *Archaeopteryx lithographica* lived. The crow-sized Archaeopteryx walked on two legs and probably glided short distances on its primitive wings. It had a head, teeth, tail, and other body parts resembling those of reptiles. But unlike reptiles, it had feathers and a wishbone, both of which are found in birds. Archaeopteryx clearly shows that reptiles and birds are related. But exactly how they are related is a matter of much debate. Some scientists think birds evolved from small dinosaurs. Others believe they evolved from other reptiles. Either way, birds, in one form or another, have lived on Earth for about 150 million years.

WHY BIRDS ARE ENDANGERED

The reasons birds are endangered vary from species to species, but the main cause is habitat loss. Habitat—food, water, shelter, and a place to raise young—is essential for any animal's survival. Yet as human population grows, more space is required for human use, for building houses, for growing food, and for other needs. Forests are cut down for firewood, furniture, chopsticks, writing paper, toilet paper, and thousands of other products. Forests are cleared so cattle can be raised on the land. Grasslands are plowed to make farm fields. Wetlands are drained so airports can be built. Houses squeeze close to coasts and riparian areas—riversides. As a result, wildlife habitat is destroyed.

Not all habitat destruction is clearly linked to the need to feed, clothe, and house more and more people. Consumer demand—people's desire to have the trappings of modern life: televisions, VCRs, computers, cars, washing machines, and other products—is a major factor, too. Many of these products require a lot of energy and materials to produce and operate. This, in turn, destroys wildlife habitat, through activities such as mining, oil drilling, coal excavation, and damming of rivers typically used to produce energy.

Was Archaeopteryx a flying reptile, or the earliest known bird? Extensive study of fossilized remains found in Germany has not yielded a definite answer.

HOW SCIENTISTS CLASSIFY BIRDS AND OTHER ORGANISMS

Scientists lump animals, plants, and other organisms into groups called classifications. The broadest categories are kingdoms. Animals belong to the animal kingdom and plants belong to the plant kingdom. Each kingdom, in turn, has a series of subgroupings: phylum, class, order, family, genus, species, and subspecies.

Birds belong to the kingdom Animalia, the phylum Chordata, and the class Aves. But the classification does not stop there. Within the class Aves, there are between twenty-eight and thirty groups called orders. (Scientists disagree about exactly how many orders there should be.) Each order has its own distinctive characteristics. One order, for instance, is the Sphenisciformes, which includes only flightless, swimming birds—the penguins. Another order is the Anseriformes—ducks, geese, and swans. The largest order is the Passeriformes, which contains perching birds, such as cardinals, robins, and blackbirds. All these orders have smaller groups within them: families, genera, species, and subspecies.

Scientists call birds and other organisms by special, scientific names. An organism's scientific name is made up of two parts: its genus and its species. For instance, *Tyto alba* is the scientific name for a barn owl because it belongs to the genus *Tyto* and the species *alba*. Some organisms also belong to a subspecies and carry that third name. Scientists worldwide, no matter what language they speak, use the same scientific names for organisms. This helps them communicate clearly about their work.

Scientists, however, sometimes disagree on the names and classifications for organisms. One scientist may think an animal belongs to one species, whereas another may think the animal belongs in another species, family, or even order. Debates and discussions such as these are constantly changing the classifications of organisms, particularly birds.

WHEN BIRDS ARE CLASSIFIED, THEY ALL HAVE THESE THREE CATEGORIES IN COMMON:

KINGDOM: Animalia

PHYLUM: Chordata

CLASS: Aves

Pollution, a by-product of many of these activities, can be a problem as well. Air pollution, water pollution, land pollution, and even noise pollution can make a habitat unlivable for birds and other wildlife. In the 1960s, the populations of ospreys, brown pelicans, and bald eagles decreased because pesticides in the birds' bodies caused the birds to lay thin-shelled eggs. When the birds incubated the eggs, sitting on them to keep them warm, the eggs collapsed. After the pesticide dichloro-diphenyl-trichloro-ethane (DDT) was banned in the United States in 1972, the thickness of the birds' eggs increased and the populations began rebounding.

An additional threat to bird populations is exotic species—species that are not native to an area. Over thousands of years, birds have adapted to cope with the animals and plants in their environment. But in the last few centuries, people have introduced new animals and plants to North America's habitats. Nonnative plants displace some native plants that produce berries, seeds, and nectars birds eat. In some cases, nonnative animals kill off native birds or compete with them for food or for nesting space. A century ago, European house sparrows and European starlings were brought into the United States by someone who wanted all the birds mentioned in Shakespeare's plays to live in North America. Today, these birds, now widespread, outcompete native birds such as wrens, bluebirds, chickadees, and hairy woodpeckers for food and nesting spots.

People's domestic cats and dogs are also major predators on birds. They disturb nests, eat eggs, kill young chicks, and even eat adult birds. According to some estimates, millions of birds are killed each year by pet cats, dogs, and other domestic animals. Feral cats and feral dogs—domestic animals that have been lost, abandoned, or released, and then become wild—are major predators on birds, as well.

Bird populations are suffering not only from exotic species, but also from certain native species that have increased dramatically. The changes people have made in the natural environment have favored the survival and spread of animals such as blue jays, raccoons, and cowbirds. Eastern North America, from the Atlantic Ocean to the Mississippi River, was once covered with a largely unbroken forest. But people cleared the land, creating a patchwork of fields, forests, and suburbia. Raccoons, blue jays, and cowbirds benefit from these changes in the landscape because they live on the edges of forests and fields. Raccoons eat bird eggs and chicks. Blue jays steal other birds' eggs from nests. Cowbirds sneak their own eggs into the nests of

Domestic animals, including pet cats, are major predators on birds, killing millions of them each year.

other birds. Cowbirds can lay dozens of eggs in one season. The nesting birds end up spending their time and energy raising cowbird chicks instead of their own!

Overharvest of birds—for food, pets, and feathers—also harms some bird populations. The Carolina parakeet and the passenger pigeon, now both extinct, were killed off, in large part, by hunters who shot them for food, for sport, and for crop protection. (The passenger pigeons laid only one egg per year, so their population quickly declined.) Some Americans are contributing to the decline of rare tropical birds by purchasing parrots and macaws caught in the wild to be pets. Such birds are smuggled illegally into the United States, and many die before they arrive at pet stores.

Without a doubt, the biggest threat to most bird species is habitat loss. But additional factors—pollution, exotic species, predators, and overharvesting—are hastening the decline of many birds, as well.

BIRDS ARE VULNERABLE   There are some reasons why birds, as a group, are vulnerable to extinction. Many species have a low reproductive rate, meaning they do not produce many offspring per year. A whooping crane, for instance, lays only two eggs, and only one of its chicks survives. A cockroach, on the other hand, can mate and produce 160 young in a year. If those young cockroaches also reproduce, and none die, in three years, those two original cockroaches could have 9,500,208,482 descendants. In the same time span, whooping cranes would have raised three chicks and no other descendants. Young whooping cranes do not even lay eggs until the age of four or five. Therefore, it's easier to wipe out a bird population than a cockroach population.

Birds, however, have one big survival advantage over many other animals: birds can fly. So why can't they fly away from the problems that threaten them? Sometimes they can. If a forest is cut down, some of the birds will fly away. But where will they go? Finding the habitat they need, including a place that is not already being occupied by some other animal, is very unlikely. Deprived of its habitat, a bird usually dies. Many birds also migrate—travel from one habitat to another regularly each year. So migrating birds depend on more than one habitat, plus the stopover sites where they rest and feed in between their seasonal homes.

WHY CARE ABOUT ENDANGERED BIRDS?   Approximately a hundred thousand species of birds have lived on Earth. Only about nine thousand of these birds species are alive today. But that is no reason to despair. Extinction is a natural process, a normal part of life. Many animals, such as dinosaurs, have evolved and died out during the course of Earth's history. Over thousands and millions of years, conditions on Earth change. Some animals adapt successfully to these changes; others do not, and become extinct.

So why are people worried about endangered animals and plants today? Because animals and plants are becoming extinct faster than ever before. Animal and plant species are dying off faster than at any other time in the last 65 million years. Scientists are very concerned that Earth is losing much of its biodiversity—its variety of animal and plant species.

Biodiversity can be important to the health of an ecosystem, a community of living organisms and the physical environment they depend on. When Earth loses animals and plants, it's like losing pieces of a puzzle, even before anyone knows where the pieces fit. Take, for example, the dodos: large birds that once lived on the island of Mauritius near the east coast of Africa. In the 1500s, dodos were killed off by sailors hunting for meat. Three hundred years later, an American scientist noticed that a beautiful tree native to the island was not reproducing. Only thirteen very old *Calvaria major* trees were left. The trees were producing seeds, but the seeds were not sprouting. The scientist wondered if the seeds needed to pass through the digestive system of a dodo in order to sprout. He tried feeding the seeds to turkeys, which have a digestive system similar to dodos. The experiment worked; several seeds sprouted! It turns out the dodo was the missing link in the tree's life cycle, just as the scientist had thought.

Many other animals and plants, like the dodo and the *Calvaria* tree, are linked. An ant, a bird, a fish, a fungus—any number of species may be important to the survival of different ecosystems, including ecosystems on which humans depend. People may not realize how important an animal is until it is gone.

Birds play essential ecological roles in the environment. Humming-birds, for instance, pollinate flowers, as bees do. Parrots spread seeds. Woodpeckers excavate holes in trees that are used later by squirrels and other animals. Forest birds eat insects, helping keep populations of tree-eating pests under control. Scientists are only beginning to understand the many complex ways birds benefit the forests, deserts, and grasslands they inhabit.

Not only are birds an indicator of ecosystem health, and an important part of the natural food web, birds are beautiful. At least many people think so and appreciate them for their gorgeous colors, shapes, and interesting behaviors. In the United States alone, 62 million people enjoy watching and feeding birds. They spend billions of dollars on bird seed each year. Obviously, feeding birds and attracting them to their yards is important to these people. For many people, the joy birds bring to their lives is yet another reason why endangered birds should be saved.

HOPE FOR BIRDS OF A FEATHER

Many serious problems threaten endangered birds. But the story of endangered birds need not be depressing. Birds are labeled "endangered" because people care enough about them to notice that the birds are in trouble and to work to ensure their survival. When people care, some bird populations can rebound.

*A*s they move from flower to flower in search of nectar, hummingbirds play an important role in pollination.

• CANARIES IN A COAL MINE? •

In the old days, before miners went down into a coal mine, they would lower a caged canary into the coal shaft and then pull it back up. If the canary was alive, the air was suitable for the miners to breathe. If the canary was dead, the mine contained poisonous gas that made mining too dangerous. Like the canary, birds in general may be an indicator of the overall health of our world.

Certain problems show up more quickly in birds than in humans. For instance, if a pesticide causes reproductive problems in animals, those problems would show up in birds the next year, when they had chicks. But in people, these reproductive problems might not show up for twenty or thirty years, when they had children. Birds also have high metabolisms, meaning their hearts beat fast, their breathing rate is rapid, and they must eat a lot of food to keep their body's energy high. Because of these factors, pesticides in the air are quickly breathed in by birds, and pesticides in insects birds eat quickly concentrate in their bodies. Their small bodies can rapidly show the effects of poisons that humans may not notice at first. For instance, people have seen whole flocks of cardinals, robins, and other birds die from breathing the air and eating the insects around lawns sprayed with pesticides just hours earlier.

If birds are sick and dying from poisons in the food they eat, the air they breathe, or the water where they swim, then the environment may be harmful for people as well. These days, people are taking notice of what birds are "telling" them and are working to solve the problems birds face. In some cases, these efforts are entirely for the sake of saving a bird species; but in other instances, bird-saving efforts have broad environmental consequences that may just help us all.

Consider the story of the snowy egret. Elegant white plumes are what gave the snowy egret its name. But beautiful feathers almost doomed these birds to extinction. In the late nineteenth century, feathers became a fashion fad. Clothing designers used the feathers of snowy egrets, herons, hummingbirds, falcons, and other birds to decorate dresses, fans, capes, hats, and muffs. Some women wore entire stuffed dead birds on their hats! An estimated five million or more birds were killed each year for the fashion trade. Snowy egrets, among the most popular source of feathers, were slaughtered in untold numbers. Soon, snowy egrets were rarely seen on the east coast of the United States, an area where they had been plentiful.

Eventually, people became concerned about the slaughter of the egrets and other birds. Many women, and a few men, began to oppose the feather business. They formed Audubon societies and began a campaign to educate people about the killing of birds for the feather trade. Eventually, wearing feathers was frowned on and feathers went out of fashion. In 1916, the United States passed the Migratory Bird Treaty Act, which gave birds some legal protection. It is the single most important law for conserving migratory birds in the United States.

After the feather trade was stopped, snowy egret populations increased. They started breeding in spots beyond their former range. Unfortunately, these avian survivors now face new threats. The wetlands where they feed and nest are being destroyed. Pesticides being used on farm fields, lawns, and other sites, are flowing into wetlands where egrets live. For these magnificent birds to survive, pollution and habitat destruction problems will have to be solved. But there's hope it can be done. As the ladies of the Audubon Society proved, if people set their minds to it, they can save rare birds.

ONE

The Fate of a Picky Eater
THE SNAIL KITE

A snail kite is the type of kite that doesn't need a string to fly. With its wings stretched wide, this graceful, hawklike bird glides over marsh wetlands such as the Everglades, a vast wetland in southern Florida. *Ka-ka-ka-ka-ka-ka* calls the kite. It dips, then tightly turns, surveying the water below for its food, apple snails.

Once a snail is spotted, the kite glides down, extends its orange legs and grabs the snail from the water plants where it feeds. Then the kite flies to a perch where it uses its long toes to hold the snail shell and its curved bill to extract the soft snail. Below the kite's perch are piles of hundreds of apple snail shells, for only occasionally will a kite eat anything else, such as a small turtle or another species of snail.

Kites belong to the family Accipitridae, the same group that includes hawks and eagles. The members of this bird family are also called birds of prey, or raptors, because they have powerful bills, legs, and talons designed for hunting and capturing animal prey. Snail kites (*Rostrhamus sociabilis*) are 16 to 18 inches (41 to 46 centimeters) long. Snail kites look like hawks, but kites have longer tails and broad, rounded wings. In the United States, snail kites live only in southern Florida wetlands. Snail kites in Florida and Cuba are a special subspecies, *Rostrhamus sociabilis plumbeus.* But other subspecies of snail kites live in Mexico and Central and South America.

Snail kites are specialists, dining almost exclusively on one kind of food, in this case, apple snails. (Generalists such as cardinals eat a variety of foods, such as seeds, insects, or fruit.) Specializing in eating apple snails has helped snail kites adapt successfully to their habitat. But in recent years, this "picky" eating habit has led to the birds' demise. In the last century, the population of apple snails drastically declined. Unlike generalists, which can shift to other food sources when one type becomes unavailable, the snail kites could not. As a result of the reduced numbers of apple snails, the snail kites have starved and died and the species has become endangered.

A BAD DAY FOR KITES Why have apple snails become so scarce? Because of the draining and destruction of Florida's wetlands, particularly the Everglades. Water once flowed south from Lake Okeechobee in a slow-moving river 50 miles (81 kilometers) wide and 6 inches (15 centimeters) or more deep. Water from this unique, sawgrass-filled river flowed southward through mangrove forests and out into Florida Bay. The entire Everglades region was a complex wilderness that was partly river, partly wetland, and partly forest.

During the last century, half of the Everglades' original 4 million acres (1,600,000 hectares) was drained to create agricultural fields and housing developments. The natural flow of water through rivers, streams, lakes, and wetlands also has been changed. Canals were dug—over 1,000 miles (1,600 kilometers) of them—to drain land, divert water to cities and farms, and control floods. South Florida's water, which once flowed through rivers and lakes, and percolated underground, came under the control of a giant, artificial plumbing system of canals, pipes, and dikes.

The loss of wetlands in south Florida killed many animals outright. Others were harmed, over the years, by the artificial plumbing system. Water levels no longer rose and fell naturally with the rainy and dry seasons. So animals and plants, which had adapted to the seasonally fluctuating water levels, died off or were forced to move elsewhere. In the last century, the number of wading birds in the Everglades has decreased by nearly 90 percent. Herons, egrets, and ibises used to nest in rookeries where hundreds of thousands of birds gathered. Now, the largest rookeries in the Everglades have only a few thousand birds. The Everglades contains thirteen species of threatened or endangered animals, including the Cape Sable seaside sparrow and the Stock Island tree snail.

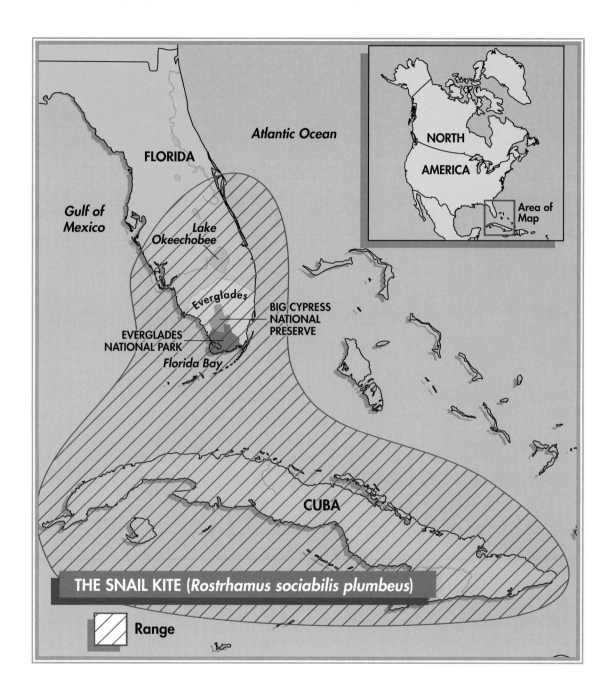

Atlantic Ocean

FLORIDA

Gulf of Mexico

Lake Okeechobee

Everglades

BIG CYPRESS NATIONAL PRESERVE

EVERGLADES NATIONAL PARK

Florida Bay

CUBA

NORTH AMERICA

Area of Map

THE SNAIL KITE (*Rostrhamus sociabilis plumbeus*)

Range

As the health of the Everglades declined, so did the number of snail kites. In many years, the Everglades received very little water at all because water was diverted to farms and cities. As a result, the land dried out and apple snails died. Snail kites starved. Worse still, when water levels are low, kites tend to nest in tall grasses instead of in trees. Kites' nests are flimsy at best. When built in the grasses, the nests often collapse. Even if the nests don't collapse, predators can easily get to the eggs or young.

These days, snail kites face additional threats. Water running off sugar-cane fields and orchards carries fertilizers and pesticides into the Everglades. Excess fertilizers from fields and sewage from cities flow into wetlands, encouraging the growth of water hyacinths and cattails. These plants clog wetlands, filling in the open water areas snail kites need for hunting.

Depending on the apple snail almost exclusively as its source of food has made the snail kite vulnerable to starvation.

KITES VERSUS STORKS   By the early 1960s, the number of snail kites in the Everglades had dropped to a low of perhaps a hundred or less. Since then, the birds have fared better, in part, because of conservation efforts being taken in the Everglades. In the last twenty years, park officials have tried hard to keep Everglades water levels high so apple snails will thrive. The snail kites, with plentiful food to eat, have increased in number. Scientists are not sure exactly how many snail kites there are, because locating and counting them all is difficult. But yearly counts, from 1985 to 1994, have ranged from a low of 326 to a high of 996.

In the meantime, however, keeping water levels high has harmed another endangered bird, the wood stork. Wood storks need low water levels, periodically, in order to raise their young in south Florida. When water levels decrease, fish crowd into smaller and smaller areas, and the wood storks can feast and feed their young more easily.

In the last decade, there has been a lot of discussion about how to manage water levels in the Everglades. Should the water levels be lowered to help wood storks or be raised to help snail kites? In the end, it was decided, the issue was not a matter of snail kites versus storks. The two bird species had coexisted for thousands of years. The decline in the overall health of the Everglades was the root of the problem. People's approach to the problem needed to change.

MORE KITES IN THE SKY   In the 1990s, progress is being made to help both kites and storks. The U.S. Fish and Wildlife Service, the U.S. Army Corps of Engineers, the South Florida Water Management District, Everglades National Park, and Big Cypress National Preserve are all working together to better manage the water system so the Everglades—with both storks and kites—can survive. If water is released at the right times, snail kites can have the water they need. They can also move around to areas where apple snails are more plentiful. Water levels will be kept low in other places, and at certain times of year, so wood storks can nest. (For a while, biologists even gave snail kites a helping hand by supporting their flimsy nests with wire baskets, to increase the birds' breeding success.)

Thanks to legislation, wood storks and snail kites may have more habitat. The Everglades National Park Protection and Expansion Act, which added 107,600 acres (43,600 hectares) to the 1.4 million-acre-(566,800 hectare-) Everglades National Park, was passed in the 1980s. And a pro-

• OLD FLINTHEAD: THE WOOD STORK •

Fortunately for wood storks, they don't have feathers on their heads and they don't taste particularly good to people. For that reason, wood storks were not killed for their feathers or for their meat by hunters who shot so many other birds at the turn of the century. Nonetheless, wood storks became endangered. The main reason was habitat loss.

Wood storks (*Mycteria americana*) are the only storks in the United States. These tall wading birds have a white body with dark, black-fringed wings and a black tail. Their heads and necks are gray and featherless, which is why some local people call them "Flintheads" or "Ironheads."

Within the southeastern United States, wood storks nest mostly in Florida, but also in Georgia, coastal South Carolina, and rarely, Alabama. Like snail kites, the wood storks in Florida are at the northern part of their range. They also live in Mexico and Central and South America.

Wood storks live in flocks. During the day, they wade through the water, probing to find small fish. Their breeding is timed so that their chicks are born during the dry parts of the year, when pools of water are shrinking and fish are easy to catch. Like snail kites, wood storks have been hurt by the changes in the Everglades ecosystem. Loss of wetlands has reduced the areas where they can live. Unnatural surges of high water, released by the man-made water control system into the Everglades, have disrupted the storks' nesting cycles. Because of these surges, the storks began nesting later in the year. Often the birds did not have enough time to raise their chicks before heavy spring rains increased water levels and made it harder to catch fish. The number of wood storks nesting in the Everglades region decreased. In 1992, only twenty-five nesting pairs were found in the park.

The good news is that these days better management of wetlands is helping wood storks. In 1996, 390 pairs nested in Everglades National Park. Wood storks have also begun nesting more often in other areas, in northern Florida, Georgia, and South Carolina. In South Carolina, the Nature Conservancy bought South Williman Island, a 2,765-acre (1,119-hectare) island that was slated for development but will now be preserved as a nesting site for wood storks and bald eagles.

WOOD STORK
Mycteria americana

   ORDER: Ciconiiformes

   FAMILY: Ciconiidae

   GENUS: *Mycteria*

   SPECIES: *americana*

Scientists, government agencies, and conservation groups have worked hard to secure a future for the Everglades snail kite.

posed "sweet" deal for the Everglades may require sugarcane growers to sell another 100,000 acres (40,500 hectares), which will be reverted to freshwater marsh. The federal government may also lower the amount of money used to subsidize Florida sugarcane growers and use that money to restore the Everglades instead. (For years, the U.S. government has subsidized the Florida sugarcane growers, giving them money and tax breaks that allow them to compete with the low-priced sugar imported from overseas.) The new program could raise $245 million for Everglades restoration. The plan has not yet been approved by Congress. But it has gained the support of the Clinton administration, Democrats in Congress, and many Republicans as well. If enacted, the plan should help restore the Everglades, benefiting both snail kites and wood storks.

TWO

BIRD OF THE FIRE

THE KIRTLAND'S WARBLER

In Michigan, mainly in Crawford, Oscoda, and Ogemaw counties, biologists are doing some very strange things. With chainsaws and logging equipment, they cut down forests and clear them. Armed with drip torches, they burn acres of land. With nets, they capture thousands of birds. Oddly enough, they do all this so a tiny, blue-gray bird with a bright yellow breast can survive. This beautiful bird is the Kirtland's warbler, an endangered species that nests nowhere else but Michigan.

WARBLER'S WORLD The Kirtland's warbler (*Dendroica kirtlandii*) was first discovered in 1851 near the Ohio farm of naturalist Jared P. Kirtland. Yet for more than fifty years, scientists did not know where Kirtland's warblers nested. In 1903, the mystery was finally solved: a naturalist discovered a Kirtland's warbler nest in Oscoda County, Michigan. Since then, most other Kirtland's warbler nests have been found within 60 miles (97 kilometers) of that first nest.

Kirtland's warblers do not spend the whole year in Michigan. In autumn they migrate to the Bahamas. After spending the winter in the Bahamas, the warblers make the taxing, 1,200-mile (1,900-kilometer) return to Michigan to nest. A little over half the birds that leave in the autumn survive to return to Michigan in the spring.

Kirtland's warblers are 6 inches (15 centimeters) long, fairly large for a warbler. Like other warblers, Kirtland's eat insects, plucking them off pine needles or snatching them in midair. They also eat blueberries and other small fruits when available. They are not "picky eaters" as snail kites are—but Kirtland's are "picky" nesters; they have very specific requirements for nesting sites.

Kirtland's warblers nest only on the ground, under a dense cover of blueberry bushes or other low shrubs, often near the bases of pine trees or small oaks. The lower branches of the pine trees help conceal their nests. However, not just any pine forest will do as a habitat. Kirtland's warblers only nest in young jack pine forests growing on sandy soil. The pine forests must have numerous, grassy, sunlit openings and be at least 80 acres (32 hectares) in size. Sandy soils are important because rainwater drains quickly through this kind of soil and does not flood the warblers' nests. The pine trees must be young, about six to twenty-two years old, and from 5 to 20 feet (1.5 to 6.2 meters) tall. Older trees lose the leafy lower branches Kirtland's need, and the habitat changes in other ways as well.

These jack pine trees need fire to reproduce. The heat of the fire opens the pine cones, and the seeds in the cones drop to the ground. Under natural conditions, lightning sparks fires that burn large areas, so jack pines can thrive. But in recent years, people have suppressed fires—putting out the fires, instead of letting them burn. Without these fires, the jack pines have not been able to reseed and sprout. This leaves the Kirtland's warblers without nesting places.

A RARE BIRD   Kirtland's warblers have probably always been fairly rare. Their native habitat, the jack pine forest on a special kind of sandy soil called Grayling soil, has never been widespread. In the last few centuries, Kirtland's warblers were probably most plentiful after lumbermen clearcut much of Michigan's forest, between 1880 and 1890. After they cut the forests, more room was left for young jack pines to grow. And back then, fires were not suppressed. As a result, forest fires raged, jack pine cones opened and released seeds, and jack pine trees sprouted and thrived. The clearcutting and fire, which were a disaster for many animal and plant species, actually helped the Kirtland's population increase.

Later, the Kirtland's habitat shrank because fires were suppressed to protect people, houses, and other property. Red pines and hardwoods were planted to replace the jack pines. Most Kirtland's warbler habitat is now found in eight counties in Michigan. This lack of habitat is one of the two major factors threatening Kirtland's warblers.

PROBLEMATIC PARASITE   The second major threat to Kirtland's warblers is brown-headed cowbirds. Cowbirds are brood parasites, meaning they lay their eggs in the nests of other species of birds. They also may remove some of the other birds' eggs to make room for their own. Not knowing they've been tricked, the host birds incubate the eggs and "adopt" the cowbird chicks, raising them as their own. Generally, the cowbird egg will hatch before the host birds' own eggs. So the cowbird gets a head start on life. Cowbird chicks grow quickly, outcompeting other chicks for food. Usually this means some, if not all, the host birds' own chicks will die. In the case of the Kirtland's warbler, only the cowbird chick survives. Meanwhile, a tiny warbler may spend all its time trying to feed a hungry cowbird chick much bigger than itself. Because a female cowbird can lay forty eggs a year, she can parasitize many nests. So even just a few cowbirds can devastate a bird population.

Here a female Kirtland's warbler feeds a cowbird chick. The warbler's own, much smaller chick is in the background.

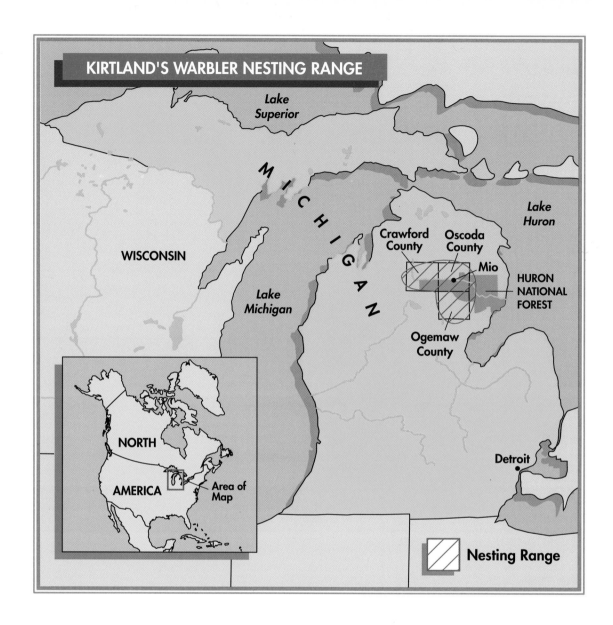

Cowbirds are native to North America. But they once lived only on the Great Plains. As people built roads and cut forests, they provided cowbirds with the fields, pastures, and forest edges where they thrive. As a result, these birds have spread all over the United States and southern Canada. They are threatening the populations of Bell's vireos, willow flycatchers, and other small birds, in addition to Kirtland's warblers.

AN AMAZING RECOVERY   In 1967, the Kirtland's warbler was declared endangered. Since then, many efforts to save the warblers have been carried out by the United States Fish and Wildlife Service, the United

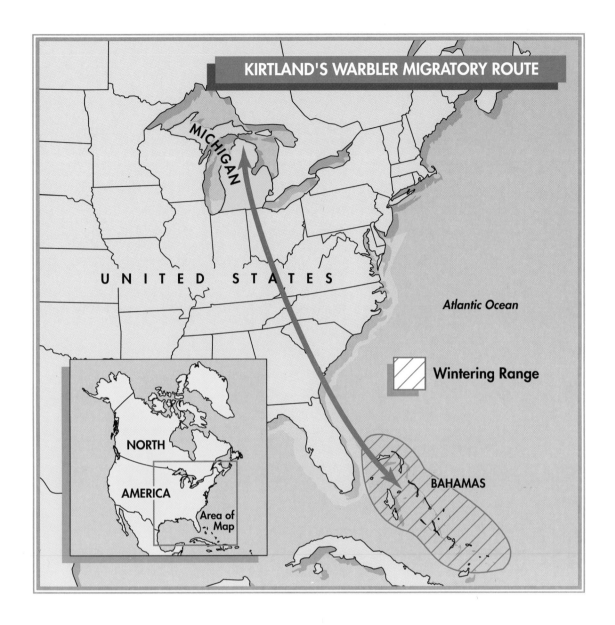

States Forest Service, the Michigan Department of Natural Resources, the Michigan National Guard, the Michigan Audubon Society, and the Michigan Natural Areas Council. Federal and state agencies bought and protected land where Kirtland's warblers nest. They have been managing forests to favor the survival of Kirtland's. This management includes planting millions of jack pine trees.

Small controlled fires, called prescribed burns, are regularly set to maintain the jack pine forest ecosystem. When trees reach fifty years of age and are big enough to be harvested for lumber, private lumbermen are allowed to purchase the trees and cut the timber off the land. In this way

*S*igns like this one warn people *away from the Kirtland's warbler nesting area near Mio, Michigan.*

both the land managers and the lumber companies profit. The land can be planted with young pines, so the Kirtland's warblers benefit, too.

To save the Kirtland's warbler, cowbirds are removed from the warbler's nesting areas. In 1994, 3,100 cowbirds were removed from the area where Kirtland's nest. (The cowbirds, when removed, are killed humanely.) So far, the program has been tremendously successful. Before cowbird trapping began, 75 percent of the Kirtland's nests were parasitized. Now that trapping is done yearly, only about 6 percent or less of Kirtland's nests are parasitized by cowbirds.

People who live near the Kirtland's warbler habitat were at first very concerned about the activities to save the warblers. They saw ugly clearcut areas and burned over areas. And a prescribed burn near Mack Lake burned

• THE CASE OF THE STOLEN EGGS •

On a snowy day in Scotland, two special investigators sit in a car. Like birdwatchers, they peer through binoculars and spotting scopes. But they're not watching birds. They are on a stakeout, watching two men they suspect may try to steal eggs.

Why would anyone steal eggs? Because in Great Britain, egg collecting is still a hobby among a small number of people. They collect fresh eggs, make a small hole in each egg, and blow out the contents. Then they keep the eggs. Like stamp collectors and coin collectors, egg collectors are passionate about their pursuit. In the 1800s, egg collecting was popular in Great Britain, Europe, and the United States. Theodore Roosevelt collected eggs. So did many famous ornithologists. But by the 1940s, egg collecting had fallen out of fashion in the United States. People were concerned about the effect collecting eggs was having on bird populations. Collecting eggs might not hurt the population of a common bird. But thousands of collectors each wanted the rarest eggs, from the rarest birds. The effect of egg collecting on these birds was probably significant.

Today, egg collecting is illegal in the United States and in England. But several hundred English egg collectors are still harming bird populations. Not long ago, investigators caught a man who had thirty-nine clutches—nestsful—of red-backed shrike eggs. These shrikes are so rare that only two pairs breed in Great Britain. They seized another man's sizable collection: twenty-six thousand eggs! Many of the eggs in these private collections are from rare or endangered species.

In the United States, where egg collecting has all but vanished, Ed Harrison is working to help the birds. Ironically, he is using egg collections to do it. In 1956, Harrison began gathering the egg collections people were giving away or throwing away because the hobby had become unpopular. He started an organization to preserve those collections and to catalog them for scientific research. Now Harrison's organization, the Western Foundation of Vertebrate Zoology, manages an eight hundred thousand egg collection in Los Angeles. Studying the eggs has helped scientists learn about the range of birds—how widespread they once were, and the number of eggs they lay. It has also helped scientists examine the relationship between egg thickness and DDT. Studying the chemical makeup of eggs may eventually help scientists understand how environmental conditions in the past differed from those of today. For all these reasons, egg collecting—the hobby that so damaged bird populations—may help them a little, after all.

Prescribed burns are an essential part of managing jack pine forests so that Kirtland's warblers will survive.

out of control, destroying some homes and businesses. Local citizens were alarmed. Government agencies involved in working to save the Kirtland's began to realize how important it was for the local community to understand and support the program, too.

Today, the burned-over land near Mack Lake is prime Kirtland's habitat and is the main reason the species is doing so well. Efforts were made to educate people in local areas and all over Michigan about the Kirtland's warbler recovery program. Birdwatchers are "flocking" to the area to see the Kirtland's warblers. U.S. Fish and Wildlife Service and U.S. Forest Service

Kirtland's warblers are a source of pride, and income, for the residents of Mio, Michigan, site of an annual Kirtland's Warbler Festival.

guides take people on tours. Local hotels, restaurants, and gift shops now cater to the tourists. People are taking pride in their local birds and benefiting from them, too. In the last few years, the town of Mio even held a "Kirtland's Warbler Festival" complete with a parade!

Currently, the recovery of the Kirtland's warbler is going extremely well. The population is censused by counting the number of singing male warblers. In 1987, only 167 singing males were recorded. But by 1993, that number was up to 485. By June 1995, 765 singing males were counted, the highest number ever. The population count decreased slightly in 1996, to 678 singing males in lower Michigan, and 14 in counties in Michigan's Upper Peninsula. If the population reaches 1,000 singing males, then the U.S. Fish and Wildlife Service will consider downlisting the species from "endangered" to "threatened" status.

THREE

TIMBER-EMBATTLED BIRD

THE RED-COCKADED WOODPECKER

North Carolina's Pinehurst Resort and Country Club is famous for its golf course. But Pinehurst has another claim to fame, living in the trees near the course's seventh hole. Red-cockaded woodpeckers, which are endangered birds, live in longleaf pines on the golf course. The owners of the resort are planting pines and ensuring that the ones where the birds already live will not be destroyed. So far, the golfers and birds appear to be coexisting peacefully. But while the golfers have been competing in friendly games, other people have been battling in court and in Congress over these woodpeckers and their fate.

A HOLE-IN-THE-WALL HOME   Red-cockaded woodpeckers (*Picoides borealis*) are small, insect-eating birds that measure about 8 inches (20 centimeters) from head to toe. They look a little bit similar to two other species, the downy woodpecker and the hairy woodpecker. But red-cockaded woodpeckers have stripes across their backs, whereas downy and hairy woodpeckers have a plain stripe going down their backs. A red tuft of feathers visible on each side of the head of the male during territorial displays gives this species its name: red-cockaded. Red-cockaded woodpeckers inhabit pine forests in the southeastern United States.

Like other woodpeckers, red-cockaded woodpeckers raise their young in holes they excavate in trees. But red-cockaded woodpeckers excavate their nesting cavities in living trees, not dead ones, as other woodpeckers do. The birds nest in pine trees, usually longleaf pines, but also loblolly pines, shortleaf pines, and other pine species. The trees must be very old, usually eighty to one hundred years old, or more. Once a tree dies, the birds abandon it. This need for old nesting trees is one of the reasons red-cockaded woodpeckers have declined. They cannot adapt to other habitats.

Nesting in a living tree has its advantages. Pine trees contain resin, a sticky liquid. (Resin is harvested from pine trees for its components—turpentine and rosin—which are used in paint thinners, paint, varnishes, shoe polishes, and other products.) Red-cockaded woodpeckers make use of this resin. A red-cockaded woodpecker will make holes around its nesting cavity so the sticky resin will flow out and cover the trunk. Each day, the bird reopens the holes so the resin flows again. Scientists suspect the birds do this because the resin discourages snakes, which could otherwise crawl into a nesting cavity and eat the eggs or baby birds. The sticky resin interferes with the snakes' movement, gluing together the scales on their bellies. So snakes rarely get past the resin barrier.

Resin may discourage snakes, but it attracts biologists. Biologists often look for the coat of sticky white resin around the nesting cavity in order to find a red-cockaded woodpecker nest. Inside the nesting cavity, the mother and father bird take turns incubating the eggs. They also share duties feeding the chicks, and brooding them—keeping them warm. Often, the parents

• WHAT'S THAT NOISE? •

Red-cockaded woodpeckers and other woodpeckers often tap their bills on trees. Why? They may be chiseling a hole, looking for insects under the bark. They may be excavating a nesting cavity. Or they may be drumming, making noise to communicate with other woodpeckers. Woodpeckers drum to declare territories and to attract mates. Sometimes, they drum just to check on one another. It's as if they were saying "Where are you?" or "I'm over here!"

also have a helper, a male bird from a previous brood. This helper may help with incubating eggs, keeping chicks warm, and even feeding the chicks. Why help? Perhaps because one day, this helper will inherit the nesting cavity where he has been helping. Nesting trees are scarce, and it takes from six months to more than four years for a bird to excavate a nesting cavity in the hard wood of living longleaf pines. So inheriting one is not a bad idea.

When a tree dies, and the resin stops flowing, red-cockaded woodpeckers abandon it. They can also sometimes be pushed out of their homes by more aggressive birds. Old nest cavities may become homes for red-bellied

Red-cockaded woodpeckers nest only in live trees, abandoning their nest tree if it dies.

woodpeckers, redheaded woodpeckers, Carolina chickadees, tufted titmice, nuthatches, flying squirrels, wood ducks, gray squirrels, or bees. More than forty animal species have been found using old red-cockaded woodpecker nesting cavities. The red-cockaded woodpecker nesting cavity, which is about 4 inches (10 centimeters) in diameter and 7 to 8 inches (18 to 20 centimeters) deep, may be enlarged by some of these later residents. By making nesting cavities that other animals use later, woodpeckers play an important role in the forest community.

TROUBLE FOR TAPPERS   Three hundred years ago, a vast belt of green forest covered almost all of the southeastern United States, from the Atlantic Coast to eastern Texas, and from Virginia to Florida. Marshes, swamps, lakes, and small clearings made by Native Americans broke up this forest. But otherwise, it was a relatively continuous tract. That's not to say all the forest looked the same. Parts were cypress swamp. Other parts were mixed deciduous forest, filled with oaks, sweetgum, maple, elm, beech, hickory, and pines. In dry, sandy soils, and where fires—set by lightning or Native Americans—were common, forests of pine grew. These pine forests were home to red-cockaded woodpeckers.

Today only minuscule patches of the old growth southeastern pine and hardwood forests remain. (Old growth forests are ones that have very old trees.) That is the problem for the two woodpeckers that needed southeastern old growth forests: the red-cockaded and the ivory-billed. The ivory-billed woodpecker, the largest woodpecker ever to live in the United States, has disappeared and is probably extinct. Red-cockaded woodpeckers are endangered. Estimates of their populations range from three thousand to nine thousand. The biggest populations exist at four sites: the Appalachicola National Forest in Florida, the Francis Marion National Forest in South Carolina, the Kisatchie National Forest in Louisiana, and the sandhills of North Carolina—on Fort Bragg and surrounding lands.

Much of what was once forest is now agricultural fields or developed areas such as highways, shopping malls, and towns. But some of it *is* forest today. Unfortunately, most of this forest is not suitable habitat for red-cockaded woodpeckers. Red-cockadeds need large areas of forest, with old trees for nesting, in order to survive. Much forest today is fragmented— broken into small patches of forest cut up by roads, clearcut patches, and so

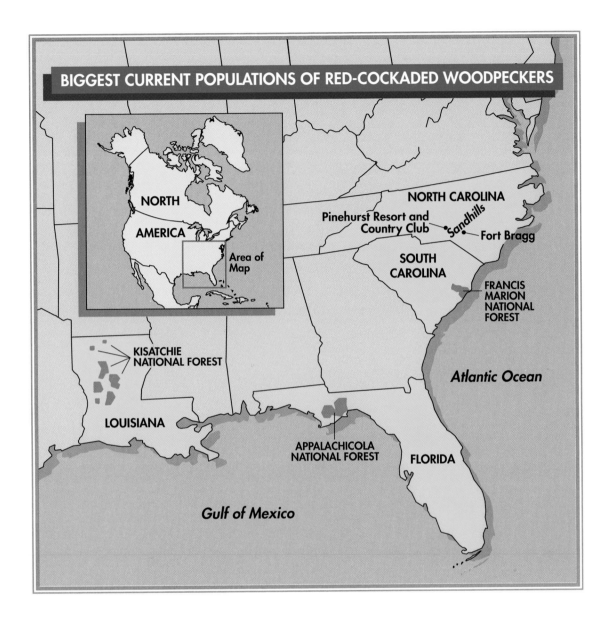

BIGGEST CURRENT POPULATIONS OF RED-COCKADED WOODPECKERS

NORTH AMERICA

Area of Map

NORTH CAROLINA

Pinehurst Resort and Country Club • Sandhills • Fort Bragg

SOUTH CAROLINA

FRANCIS MARION NATIONAL FOREST

KISATCHIE NATIONAL FOREST

LOUISIANA

Atlantic Ocean

APPALACHICOLA NATIONAL FOREST

FLORIDA

Gulf of Mexico

on. Little of the forest contains enough old pines for red-cockaded wood-peckers to thrive.

At the turn of the century, southeastern forests were harvested for tim-ber. So most of the forest we see today is what has regrown after the primary forest was cut. Pines are among the first trees to regrow on these cutover plots. But through a natural process called succession, deciduous trees such as oaks and hickories can eventually take over the forest. The oaks, hickories, and sweetgums shade out the pines, making conditions unsuitable for them.

Pines can only outcompete other trees where soils are nutrient-poor or fires sweep through frequently. Normally, lightning-sparked fires occasionally burn many southeastern forests, killing oaks, hickories, and most other trees. Thick, fire-resistant bark and, in older trees, tree branches high above the ground help protect pines from being harmed. Just as with the jack pines described in Chapter Two, fires are essential for pines. The fires heat their cones, causing them to open and drop seeds.

As Chapter Two explained, in the last century, people have suppressed natural fires, putting them out before they could burn the forests. As a result, in parts of the southeastern United States, the oaks and hickories have thrived instead of the pines. People have also planted tree farms of pines. But many are harvested before they are old enough to serve as nest trees for red-cockaded woodpeckers. So the main problem for these birds, as it is for so many others, is habitat loss, caused by timber harvest, forest fragmentation, and fire suppression.

WOODPECKER WARS   Saving a small area of trees on a golf course is not going to ensure that red-cockaded woodpeckers, as a species, survive. At best, it's a stopgap measure. In the wild, one clan—one family group of red-cockaded woodpeckers—inhabits a home of 125 to more than 1,000 acres (51 to 405 hectares). Red-cockaded woodpeckers do best in the middle of large tracts of forest. Near the edges of forests, or clearings where patches have been clearcut, other kinds of birds dominate the scene. Flickers, starlings, and redheaded woodpeckers take over red-cockaded woodpecker nesting cavities. So plenty of land must be set aside to preserve the species.

The red-cockaded woodpecker was declared an endangered species in 1969. Since then, efforts to save the species have been complicated by politics and controversy. During the 1970s and early 1980s, a national recovery team was organized—a team of people who were to make plans to ensure the survival of the red-cockaded woodpecker. The team met repeatedly, and in the end they agreed on a plan. But the plan was never implemented. Lumber companies were worried that rules created by the team would limit their harvest of timber on both their own private lands and forest service lands. The U.S. Forest Service, which controls some of the United States' publicly held reserves of timber, was concerned that safeguarding the red-cockaded woodpeckers would reduce the harvest of timber too much. This would reduce the U.S. Forest Service's and lumber companies' revenues. Mean-

The Pinehurst Resort and Country Club has joined in the effort to save red-cockaded woodpecker habitat.

while, biologists were seeing the red-cockaded woodpecker populations decline. They, and many environmentalists, felt the red-cockaded woodpeckers were not being properly protected.

The controversy, in many ways, mirrored the troubles going on in the Pacific Northwest over the threatened spotted owl and the Pacific old growth forests on which they depend. In both cases, the birds depended on old growth forests that lumber companies wanted to harvest from public lands such as national forests. And in both cases, environmentalists tried to block these timber-harvest plans.

All the while, new studies were showing rapid woodpecker population declines in Texas, Florida, and South Carolina. Then, in 1989, Hurricane Hugo hit South Carolina, destroying most of the woodpecker nesting cavi-

Hurricane Hugo devastated South Carolina's Francis Marion National Forest, one of four major red-cockaded woodpecker nesting areas.

ties in Francis Marion National Forest, where one-quarter of all red-cockaded woodpeckers lived. For red-cockaded woodpeckers, things seemed dark indeed.

SAFE HARBORS AND OTHER SOLUTIONS
Today, scientists believe that the best hope for the survival of red-cockaded woodpeckers is to properly manage national forest lands, where more than half of all the red-cockaded woodpeckers live. A landmark court case in 1989 made better management more likely. The Sierra Club Legal Defense Fund and other environmentalists sued the U.S. Forest Service, claiming they were violating the Endangered Species Act by carrying out timber harvest that damaged red-cockaded woodpecker habitat. The court ruled that the U.S. Forest Service would have to change its ways and protect the woodpeckers. Since then, some progress has been made toward managing timber harvests so that pine trees are left standing long enough to serve as woodpecker nesting sites. The trees in some sites will only be harvested every 100 to 120 years. Forests will also be burned on a regular schedule, to suppress other trees and to favor the pines. This new management plan will help more than just woodpeckers. According to the U.S. Fish and Wildlife Service, 167 other endangered, threatened, and rare plant and animal species will benefit as well.

After Hurricane Hugo's devastation, biologists in South Carolina gave red-cockaded woodpeckers a head start at recovery. Biologists helped construct new nesting cavities for the woodpeckers. They took large chunks of wood and drilled the proper-sized nesting cavities in them. Then they attached these wood chunks, with ready-made cavities, to old pines. Woodpeckers soon moved in. Although 63 percent of the woodpeckers were gone from the Francis Marion National Forest after the hurricane, building nesting cavities and other efforts to improve the habitat have helped the population there to recover.

To increase woodpecker reproduction, biologists have begun transplanting juvenile females to clusters that contain adult males. This woodpecker "dating service" has been quite successful, so far. Many of the transplanted birds have successfully "pair-bonded" with prospective mates. Some of the transplants brought together woodpeckers from widely separated populations. This may help increase genetic diversity, the variation in the

Inserting artificial nesting cavities (inset) into old pines is one way to replace those damaged by storms and improve habitat for red-cockaded woodpeckers.

birds' genes. A variety of genes can make for stronger, healthier populations overall.

Even the military has pitched in to help woodpeckers. Military bases have some of the best wildlife habitats around, because they have been protected from logging, grazing, and other development over the years. In the southeastern United States, some bases have extensive pine forests. (Fires, touched off by exploding bombs at target ranges and practice sites, have burned the forests and favored the growth of pines.) Recently, Eglin Air Force Base in Florida and other military bases began managing their habitats to promote wildlife diversity. Their troop training still goes on. But red-cockaded woodpecker nesting trees are marked, and troops try to avoid them. Eglin Air Force Base is also a haven for many other endangered, rare, and threatened species.

Other experimental efforts to protect red-cockaded woodpeckers are being undertaken. Today, through a government program called "Safe Harbor," private landowners are encouraged to plant longleaf pines and maintain them as red-cockaded habitat. However, the landowners are allowed to do whatever they want with their habitats in the future. Previously, according to the U.S. Fish and Wildlife Service, some private landowners avoided planting longleaf pines, because if endangered red-cockaded woodpeckers settled in, the landowners would have to get government permission to cut the trees. The U.S. Fish and Wildlife Service is hoping that the habitat will exist long enough to help the woodpeckers.

Pinehurst Golf Course signed up to be the first "Safe Harbor" for woodpeckers. They are planting pines and installing artificial nesting cavities for the woodpeckers. A private landowner in Fayetteville, North Carolina, is also signed up for the Safe Harbor program. He's growing longleaf pine trees so he can rake up the pine straw they create and sell it for gardener's mulch. Other landowners can plant the trees, with an eye on timber harvest a long time down the road. These landowners are justifiably proud of their conservation efforts. Some old trees are protected. And if the newly planted ones are allowed to grow for seventy to one hundred years, they may become nesting trees for red-cockaded woodpeckers.

Will the Safe Harbor program work? People differ in their opinions. Many U.S. Forest Service employees, lumber companies, and private landowners think Safe Harbor is a terrific idea and a wonderful compromise.

A wildlife biologist captures and tags a red-cockaded woodpecker on private land in the Sandhills of North Carolina.

But some biologists are concerned that the Safe Harbor program is just an excuse not to protect red-cockaded woodpecker habitats elsewhere. Some would even go so far as to say it's a publicity stunt and a weakening of the Endangered Species Act. They doubt whether the landowners will keep the trees growing long enough to benefit the woodpeckers.

It is unclear whether, in the long run, Safe Harbor will help red-cockaded woodpeckers survive. Fortunately, other conservation programs in national forests and on military bases are also being carried out. With so many people working to ensure that these birds have the habitat they need, red-cockaded woodpeckers have a good chance of survival.

FOUR

BEACHGOERS VERSUS BIRDS

THE PIPING PLOVER

Piping plovers, except for the male during breeding season, are the color of the sand where they live. If it weren't for their constant piping calls, *peep!* or *peep-lo!* or *pee-a-weet!* or *per-wee!*, many people would not know the birds were there at all. No wonder some drivers of dune buggies and jeeps may not see the plover chick that occasionally gets crushed underneath their tires. Other people, however, *are* taking notice of plovers and the plight of this endangered bird. These days, some plovers even get their own private beaches: long stretches of shoreline closed to humans so these delicate, scurrying birds can nest in peace.

PLOVERS AND THEIR PROBLEMS
Piping plovers (*Charadrius melodus*) are small, 7¼ inch (almost 18½ centimeter) shorebirds. They live on sandy, gravelly, or pebbly beaches, next to oceans, lakes, or occasionally, even streams. Usually these birds nest on the flat, sandy, bare areas between dunes. Piping plovers breed on North America's Atlantic Coast from North Carolina to Quebec. They also breed inland, on the shores of the Great Lakes and large lakes in the prairies of Minnesota and parts of Canada. In autumn, piping plovers migrate to the southeastern Atlantic Coast of the United States, the Gulf Coast of Texas, as well as islands in the Caribbean.

Piping plovers, wherever they occur, have been in decline for decades. In the late 1800s and early 1900s, they were hunted for feathers used to decorate hats. Once feathered hats went out of fashion, piping plover populations began to recover. But then habitat destruction and degradation—the decreasing quality of habitats—began to take their toll.

Beaches and dunes, once quiet spots where plovers could nest, have gradually become crowded with people. Houses, roads, and boardwalks have been built over dunes. This leaves less space for piping plovers to nest. Many shores have also been stabilized with seawalls, jetties, and groins installed to protect buildings and beaches from erosion. Ironically, these structures have ultimately led to the overall erosion and disappearance of beaches all along the coast. They interfere with the natural flow of sand from beach to beach, starving some beaches of sand and steepening others.

On the remaining beaches, the main threat to plovers is off-road vehicles such as dune buggies and jeeps. These vehicles tear up plover habitat. Chicks fall into tire tracks, and the vehicles crush chicks and eggs.

Beachcombers, too, disturb piping plovers. Studies show that when people come near their nesting grounds, piping plovers fly up in defense. As a result, the plovers spend their time defending their territories instead of incubating eggs or feeding their chicks. Even flying kites on strings can startle the birds into believing flying predators are nearby. Unleashed dogs and cats can kill chicks, eat eggs, and disturb the nesting birds. Plus, garbage left by beach visitors attracts raccoons, foxes, skunks, opossums, and rats, all of which will also eat eggs and chicks.

All these problems have led to a drastic decrease in the number of piping plovers. What was once a common bird has decreased to the point of scarcity. By 1986, 80 percent of the sites where plovers once nested in Manitoba, Canada, were empty. Only a few dozen lived near the Great Lakes. From Maine to North Carolina, only eight hundred breeding pairs of piping plovers could be found.

BENEFITING FROM BEACHES

Sometimes a species may become scarce in part of its range but be more plentiful in other locales. The Endangered Species List accounts for these differences by listing populations separately. That is the case with piping plovers. The populations that nest along the Atlantic Coast and in the northern Great Plains are consid-

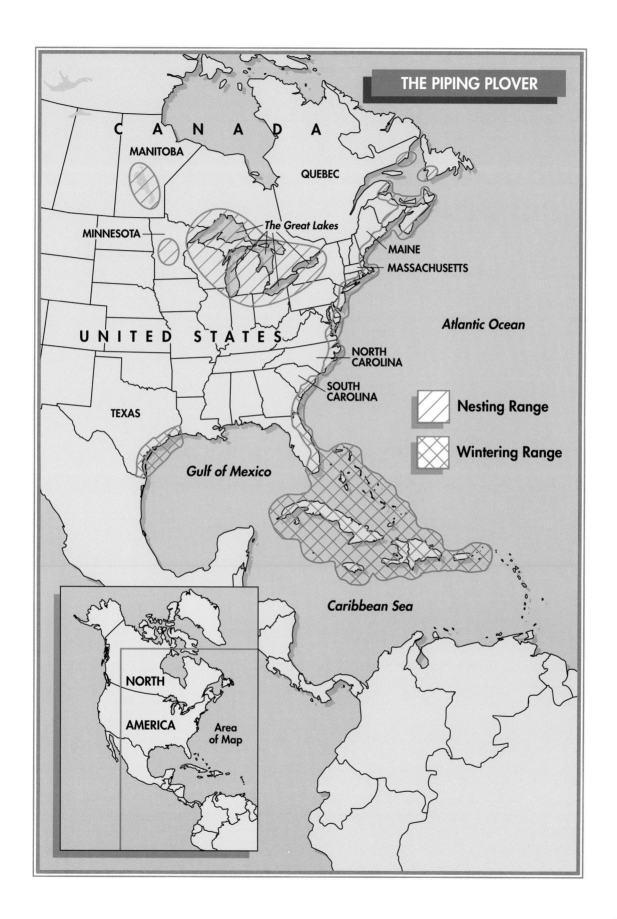

THE PIPING PLOVER

CANADA

MANITOBA

QUEBEC

MINNESOTA

The Great Lakes

MAINE

MASSACHUSETTS

UNITED STATES

Atlantic Ocean

NORTH
CAROLINA

SOUTH
CAROLINA

Nesting Range

Wintering Range

TEXAS

Gulf of Mexico

Caribbean Sea

NORTH

AMERICA   Area
of Map

Another endangered resident of beaches is the least tern (*Sterna antillarum*). Least terns nest among pebbles, shells, or short grasses on beaches by lakes, rivers, or oceans. Their nests are not much more than scraped away spots where they lay their eggs. To feed themselves and their chicks, these graceful hunters hover above the water, then dive and snatch fish, insects, and crabs.

Least terns were once fairly common, ranging along beaches on both the Pacific and Atlantic coasts of the United States, as well as Mexico, and along Caribbean shores. They also nest on inland beaches as far north as South Dakota. As its name indicates, the least tern is North America's smallest tern, only 8.5 to 9.5 inches (21.6 to 24.1 centimeters) long. The species is divided into three subspecies, two of which were declared endangered in 1985. About 4,500 least terns remained in 1987.

ered threatened. But the population that lives along the Great Lakes is considered endangered.

Piping plovers have made a remarkable recovery in certain areas. In the last ten years, the number of nesting pairs has increased from 800 to 1,150 along the Atlantic coast of the United States. (To be taken off the endangered species list, this population needs to rise to two thousand breeding pairs.) Massachusetts is the key to this success story—the place where most

As many as one hundred thousand least terns were killed per year at the height of the feather trade, around 1900. Almost wiped out by this hunting, the population now faces other threats. Sandbars and shores where terns nest have been destroyed by the damming of rivers. Like piping plovers, least tern eggs and nests are vulnerable to predators such as cats, rats, and raccoons. They are also disturbed by beachgoers. Plans to help the least tern recover include the creation of fenced-off, artificial nesting sites.

LEAST TERN
Sterna antillarum
> **ORDER:** Charadriiformes
> **FAMILY:** Laridae
> **GENUS:** *Sterna*
> **SPECIES:** *antillarum*

of the gains have been made. (In the southern part of their range, piping plover numbers decreased or remained the same.) In 1986, Massachusetts had 139 breeding pairs; by 1995, there were 447. The increases in Massachusetts are likely due to the closing of selected beaches to off-road vehicles such as dune buggies.

Closing beaches to off-road vehicles has not been the only action taken to help piping plovers. Park rangers have also been educating beachgoers

Piping plovers need quiet beaches and dunes where they can nest and hatch their chicks.

about the importance of not disturbing the birds. Nesting areas have been fenced off to keep out predators. Pets, and in some cases, pedestrians have been banned from beach areas near known nesting spots. Eroding beaches have been stabilized to maintain habitat for the birds.

The future looks good for piping plovers. But off-road vehicle enthusiasts are outspoken in their desire to have beaches reopened for them. There is talk of opening more plover nesting areas to vehicle traffic in Massachusetts.

Like so many other endangered species, piping plovers are an indicator of the health of the beach habitat in general. If they recover and their beach homes are protected, other rare, beach-dwelling species may benefit as well. These beach-dwellers and visitors include the threatened northeastern beach tiger beetle, the threatened loggerhead sea turtle, the threatened and endangered populations of roseate terns, and a threatened plant called the seabeach amaranth.

FIVE

BACK FROM THE BRINK
THE WHOOPING CRANE

To save endangered whooping cranes, people will do some seemingly zany things. In Wisconsin, a woman dresses up in a whooping crane costume. In Canada, a man wades through waist-deep water to sneak an egg out of a nest. In Idaho, a pilot flies an ultralight plane 800 miles (1,290 kilometers), with seven young cranes flying behind, in formation. All these people are helping to ensure the survival of whooping cranes, one of the most endangered bird species on Earth.

THE CALL OF THE CRANES   Tall, long-legged, graceful in flight, cranes belong to the scientific family Gruidae, also known as the crane family. They are closely related to rails and coots but not to storks and herons, as you might expect.

The world's fifteen crane species are revered in many cultures. In Greek and Roman tradition, cranes were considered wise, generous, kind birds. In Japan and China, cranes are symbols of happiness and long life. In Europe and Asia, people once imitated the hopping, wing-flapping courtship dances of cranes as part of yearly rituals to welcome spring and help crops grow.

Whooping cranes (*Grus americana*) live only in North America. The name "whooping" crane refers to their resonant call, which can be heard from several miles away. The tallest birds in North America, whooping cranes stand 4 to 5 feet (1.2 to 1.5 meters) tall and have a wingspan of 7 to 8 feet (2 to 2.4 meters). Adult cranes have snowy white bodies, black-tipped

WHOOPING CRANE
Grus americana

ORDER: Gruiformes
FAMILY: Gruidae
GENUS: *Grus*
SPECIES: *americana*

wings, and long black legs. Red, bare skin patches crown their heads and mark their cheeks.

Whooping cranes live in wet, grassy areas such as freshwater marshes, wet prairies, and edges of lakes. Wading through shallow water, cranes probe the mud for crayfish and other crustaceans. They pluck fish out of the water and pick insects, berries, and grain off plants.

In April or May, whooping cranes arrive at their nesting grounds. The males set up territories—places they defend against other male whooping cranes. Hopping, wing-flapping dances are performed by the males and females during courtship. Once they have bonded, male and female whooping cranes stay together for life. (They can live about twenty-five years in the wild.) The pair mates and builds a round, heaping nest of grass or reeds on the ground in the wetland. The female lays two eggs, but usually only one chick survives. After nesting season in mid-September, whooping cranes begin migrating south to warmer locales for the winter.

FROM HISTORY TO MYSTERY

Whooping cranes were once widespread in wet areas of North America, from the midwest to the southeastern United States, and as far west as Utah's Great Salt Lake. They also lived in central Canada, from the U.S. border to the Arctic Circle, and in Mexico. But in the last few centuries, wetlands and prairies were converted to farmlands. Cranes, which are shy birds, were disturbed by settlers. By 1865, only an estimated 700 to 1,400 whooping cranes remained. Habitat loss continued and hundreds of whooping cranes were killed by hunters for trophies, museum specimens, and egg collections. By 1941, there were only sixteen birds left.

Those sixteen birds belonged to a single flock, which spent the winter at Aransas National Wildlife Refuge on the Gulf Coast of Texas. No one knew where they spent the summers; where they nested was a mystery. It was not until 1954 that the nesting grounds of the whooping cranes were discovered in Wood Buffalo National Park , which straddles the border of Alberta and the Northwest Territories of Canada. In autumn, the whooping cranes make a 2,500-mile (4,000-kilometer) journey back to Aransas National Wildlife Refuge.

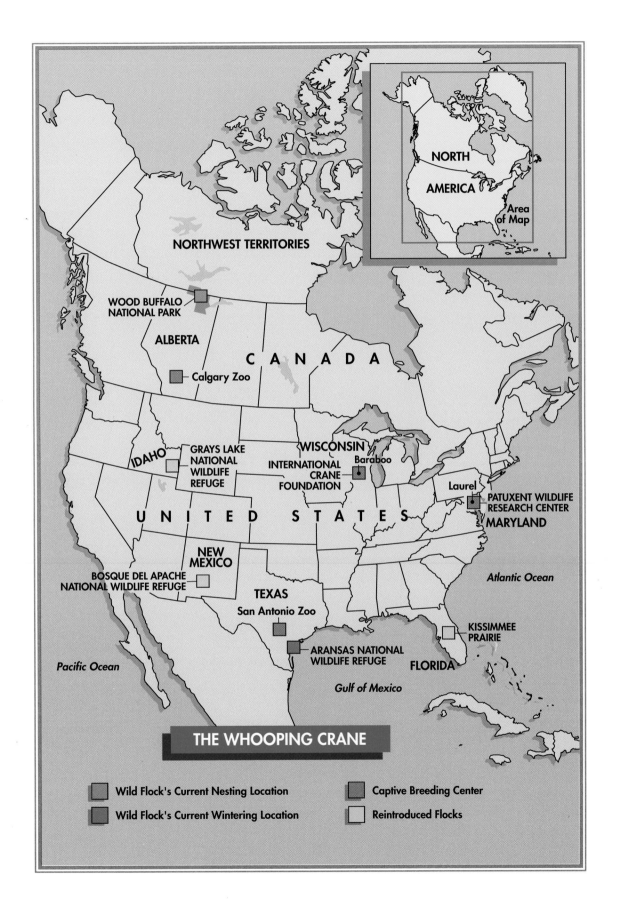

NORTHWEST TERRITORIES

WOOD BUFFALO
NATIONAL PARK

ALBERTA

C A N A D A

Calgary Zoo

IDAHO

GRAYS LAKE
NATIONAL
WILDLIFE
REFUGE

WISCONSIN

Baraboo

INTERNATIONAL
CRANE
FOUNDATION

Laurel

PATUXENT WILDLIFE
RESEARCH CENTER

MARYLAND

U N I T E D   S T A T E S

NEW
MEXICO

BOSQUE DEL APACHE
NATIONAL WILDLIFE REFUGE

TEXAS

San Antonio Zoo

Atlantic Ocean

KISSIMMEE
PRAIRIE

ARANSAS NATIONAL
WILDLIFE REFUGE

FLORIDA

Pacific Ocean

Gulf of Mexico

NORTH

AMERICA

Area
of Map

THE WHOOPING CRANE

Wild Flock's Current Nesting Location

Wild Flock's Current Wintering Location

Captive Breeding Center

Reintroduced Flocks

63

CAPTIVE BREEDING   Scientists know that whooping cranes typically lay two eggs each year, but usually only one of the chicks that hatches survives. So in 1967, scientists working to restore the whooping crane population began taking a single egg out of each crane nest and raising it in captivity. By removing the egg, scientists did no harm and hoped to do some good.

Raising the cranes has proven challenging, even though scientists spent seven years practicing by working with sandhill cranes—a more common crane species—before attempting to work with the scarce whooping cranes. Using a special machine that keeps the eggs at the right temperature and turns them daily, scientists are able to carefully incubate the eggs. Once a chick hatches, the two main challenges are making sure the bird eats and that it imprints on cranes. Imprinting is a process young birds go through in the first few weeks of their lives. They imprint on their parents, meaning they follow their parents around and imitate them. If imprinting occurs properly, when the birds mature, they will look for a bird of their own species with which to mate. However, in the first few weeks, a bird without a parent may imprint on a different animal. Ducks and cranes have been known to imprint on people and follow them around! If a young crane imprints on a human, it is unlikely it will ever form a pair-bond with another crane and successfully reproduce.

To prevent captive whooping cranes from imprinting on people, biologists do a variety of things. When feeding the birds, the caretakers do not allow the birds to see them. The animal care specialists hide behind fences or screens. They wear crane puppets on their hands when feeding the cranes. Using a puppet, they peck at the food in a bowl, teaching the young crane to feed. The young whooping cranes are also placed in cages next to adult whooping cranes so they will see others of their own species. As the birds mature, they are cared for by keepers who dress in whooping crane costumes. This helps insure the birds will never learn to like or trust humans, which is important if these birds are to survive in the wild.

It was at Patuxent Wildlife Research Center, near Laurel, Maryland, where scientists first raised enough chicks to form a sizable flock. But the whooping cranes were not mating. So scientists added a little "mood lighting." They rigged lights to mimic the long summer days of bright light that the whooping cranes experience in Canada at their breeding grounds. (Maryland has fewer hours of daylight than occur in Canada during the

Animal care specialists wear crane puppets on their hands when feeding young cranes to prevent the birds from imprinting on humans.

cranes' breeding season.) The experiment worked and some of the cranes mated. Female whooping cranes who did not mate through normal means were artificially inseminated. Sperm from a male crane was injected into them so their eggs would be fertilized. Then, to improve the hatching of cranes, biologists sneaked a single whooping crane egg out of each of the whooping crane nests. But this time, the "extra" eggs were not incubated by scientists in captivity. They were slipped into the nests of wild sandhill cranes, in place of the sandhills' eggs. The wild sandhill cranes raised the baby whooping cranes.

To establish a second captive population of whooping cranes, biologists took twenty-two whooping cranes from Patuxent and transferred them to the International Crane Foundation in Baraboo, Wisconsin, in 1989. Later, a captive population was started at the Calgary Zoo in Calgary, Canada. By 1995, captive whooping crane populations included fifty-seven whooping cranes at Patuxent, thirty-one whooping cranes at the International Crane Foundation, sixteen at the Calgary Zoo, and four at the San Antonio Zoo in Texas.

• THE MAN WHO DANCED WITH A CRANE •

When he was six years old, George Archibald liked chickens. By his preteen years, he had pet ducks. In high school, he helped local wildlife officials hatch ring-necked pheasants to introduce into the wild. So no one should have been too surprised when he eventually chose a career studying birds.

Archibald grew up in Nova Scotia, much of the time on a family farm. After attending college at Canadian universities, he went to graduate school at Cornell, in Ithaca, New York. There he studied cranes' calls and met Ron Sauey, another student. Together, the two "hatched" a seemingly crazy plan to save the world's cranes.

At the time, almost half the world's crane species were endangered. Sauey and Archibald decided they would try to breed the cranes in captivity and help preserve wild habitat. They talked Sauey's father into letting them establish a crane breeding center on his horse farm in Baraboo, Wisconsin. In 1972, the two friends began their dream, establishing an organization to protect cranes worldwide.

The going wasn't always easy, and funding was sometimes scarce, but today, their organization, the International Crane Foundation (ICF), is a thriving nonprofit organization. It works with organizations in India, Japan, China, Vietnam, South Korea, South Africa, Russia, Myanmar, and many other countries to protect crane species and their habitats. Many species of cranes are bred in captivity on the organization's grounds in Wisconsin. ICF has been involved in the captive breeding of many cranes, including whooping cranes in North America. In fact, one of the most famous episodes in captive crane conservation involves George Archibald and a crane named Tex.

Tex was a whooping crane that was born in captivity. But unfortunately, all she saw in her first few weeks of life was humans. So rather than imprinting on her parents, she imprinted on humans. When Tex grew up, she looked for humans to mate with, instead of cranes!

By 1976, Tex was nine years old. She was one of the few whooping cranes left in the world. Yet she had not produced an egg. It was important that she do so, so her genes would be passed on to other cranes. Tex was one of the few descendants of a flock of Louisiana cranes that had been wiped out in the wild. That is why serious scientists decided it was time for Archibald to dance with Tex.

In the wild, cranes dance in order to reinforce the pair-bond with their mates. The dancing and courting signals the female's body to get ready to breed. When she is ready, the birds mate and the female's eggs are fertilized inside her body. Captive cranes don't need to mate. Females can be artificially inseminated with sperm from males. But first, the females must be in breeding condition—their body must be releasing eggs for fertilization.

Tex's body never got ready for breeding because she thought she should mate with people, not cranes. So to get her into breeding condition, George Archibald lived twenty-four-hours a day with Tex. He lived in a shack in her pen. He wore a red cap, just in case it would make him a little more attractive to Tex. He even danced the whooping crane dance, making calls and flapping his arms like a crane. Tex responded by dancing, too.

Archibald's efforts were successful. Tex formed a pair-bond with him. (She even chased away female humans that visited Archibald in the field.) Eventually, Tex came into breeding condition and was artificially inseminated with genetic material from a male whooping crane. She laid an egg that year, and more in several years afterward. But those eggs did not produce healthy chicks.

Over several years, Archibald and other scientists spent time living and dancing with Tex during breeding seasons. In 1982, George and Tex danced their dance once again. And finally, that year, Tex laid an egg that hatched, and the chick survived. The chick, an amazing product of a truly incredible experiment, was appropriately named Gee Whiz.

Unfortunately, just a few weeks after Gee Whiz was born, Tex was killed by a raccoon. So Archibald no longer needs to dance with cranes. But his work, and ICF's work on crane conservation, continues today.

George Archibald's outstanding efforts led to the birth of Tex's first and only chick.

WHEN ARE THERE TOO FEW LEFT TO SAVE?

In 1941, there were only sixteen whooping cranes left. There were so few remaining that there was little hope of saving the cranes. A small population of animals, particularly if it is located in one place, is vulnerable. A storm, disease outbreak, or other such event can easily wipe out the whole group. For example, a storm in 1940 wiped out six of the thirteen whooping cranes living in Louisiana's White Lake area. In later years, disease outbreaks from mosquito-borne viruses and contaminated food killed captive whooping cranes. Another problem of small populations is lack of genetic diversity and inbreeding.

Individual animals of the same species may look alike to humans. But each one is genetically different, meaning they have a different set of genes. (Except for identical twins or clones, which are genetically identical.) These genes are molecules that contain the instructions that determine traits such as eye color, feather shape, and the body's resistance to disease. Genetic diversity, a variety of genes, gives a population a better chance of survival. Why? Because if environmental conditions change, a diverse population is more likely to have the genes needed to adapt. For example, if a disease breaks out, a variety of genes means there's a better chance some of the animals will be resistant to the disease.

An additional problem with small populations is inbreeding. Inbreeding occurs when an animal mates with a close relative of the same species. (A closely related animal will have similar genes.) Offspring created by inbreeding have an increased risk of birth defects, deformities, or susceptibility to disease. That is because these offspring are more likely to have two copies of any "bad" or negative genes—one from each parent. So the negative results of these genes show up, or are intensified. Many wild animals have behaviors that help them avoid inbreeding. Young animals, for instance, may travel far from their families before finding a mate. In this way, inbreeding is avoided. But when only a few animals are left, as with the whooping cranes and California condors, some degree of inbreeding is unavoidable. Inbreeding may make future generations less likely to survive.

WHOOPERS IN THE WILD

Part of the plan to help whooping cranes recover involves establishing wild flocks in several different areas of North America. Working toward that end in 1975, biologists placed whooping crane eggs in the nests of sandhill cranes at Grays Lake National Wildlife Refuge in Idaho. The sandhill cranes successfully raised the whooping crane chicks, who migrated with their foster parents to Bosque del Apache National Wildlife Refuge in New Mexico. But the young whooping cranes imprinted on sandhill cranes. So when they reached breeding age, they tried to mate with sandhill cranes, not whooping cranes. One pair produced what scientists have nicknamed a "whoophill," a whooping crane/sandhill crane hybrid.

Over the years, most of the whooping cranes at this site died or were killed by disease and collisions with power lines. Coyotes killed some of the younger cranes, too. By 1996, only three adult whooping cranes were still part of the wild flock at Grays Lake National Wildlife Refuge.

Currently, the goal of the U.S. Fish and Wildlife Service is to establish and maintain three wild flocks of whooping cranes. A flock that winters in Texas and spends the summer in Canada will be increased to forty pairs by adding captive-bred birds. A second flock is being established at Florida's Kissimmee Prairie. These birds, presumably, will not migrate because they will not be taught to do so.

In February 1993, fourteen young, captive-bred whooping cranes were released at the Kissimmee Prairie. Nine were killed by bobcats. More cranes have been added each year since then. By August 1996, fifty-two inhabited the site. A third flock of migratory whooping cranes will be started somewhere else; the site has not yet been determined.

MORE WILD FLIGHTS

In the autumn of 1995, seven sandhill cranes flew behind an ultralight aircraft from Grays Lake National Wildlife Refuge to their winter home in Bosque del Apache National Wildlife Refuge. The 800-mile (1,290-kilometer) trip took eleven days, with stopovers to rest and feed. Why were the cranes following the plane? Because when they were young, the cranes were imprinted on the sight and sound of the ultralight plane, as well as on other cranes. If the sandhill crane experiment is successful and the cranes follow the migratory route on their own the next year, this technique may be used to teach whooping cranes to migrate to a certain place.

• CAPTIVE BREEDING •
SENSATIONAL SUCCESS OR EXPENSIVE FAILURE?
THE CALIFORNIA CONDOR

Two hundred years ago, gigantic birds with a 10-foot (3-meter) wingspan soared over the west coast of North America, from Baja California to British Columbia, and parts of Arizona, Utah, New Mexico, and Texas. These majestic birds, California condors (*Gymnogyps californianus*), scavenged carcasses of dead animals.

Over the last two centuries, the birds declined in number, partly because people hunted and killed off many of the herd animals condors eat. Hunters also shot the condors and collected their eggs. And condors died from eating poisoned carcasses intended to kill coyotes. These and other factors led to their decline. By April 1985, only six California condors were left. The U.S. Fish and Wildlife Service decided to take those into captivity to try to breed them. In 1987 the last wild California condor was captured.

The decision to capture the condors was controversial. Some people believed the animals should be allowed to die in the wild, in dignity, instead of being taken into captivity. They did not want the birds to be subjected to the poking and prodding and laboratory conditions of captive animals. Others felt it was useless to spend so much money on a virtually hopeless case—trying to save these animals, when so few were left. (With only six condors remaining, there was little genetic diversity in the population.) Still others felt that once the birds were in captivity, there would be little incentive to protect their habitat in the wild. And some conservationists felt the money could be better spent by setting aside land so that other species, with more of a chance, could survive.

Despite these concerns, captive breeding of California condors began. The U.S. Fish and Wildlife Service, the San Diego Wild Animal Park, and the Los Angeles Zoo have worked together on the project. It has been complicated and expensive, a program that costs about $1.5 million per year.

Using captive breeding techniques similar to those for whooping cranes, biologist were able to increase the California condor population to 103 birds in early 1996. Yet the problem remains that their natural habitat is still as dangerous for them today as it was when they were taken from the wild. Nevertheless, biologists have been working to release California condors into the wild. First, biologists practiced release techniques using Andean condors, which are relatively plentiful in captivity and in the wild. Then, in 1992 and 1993, thirteen captive-bred California condors were released. Four died when they collided with utility poles and power lines. One died after drinking from a puddle of antifreeze it found in a parking lot.

Biologists knew they had to train the next condors they released to avoid these dangers. To teach them to avoid power poles, biologists set up a fake power pole in the condor cage. The pole had a low-voltage wire that would mildly shock the condors if they landed on it. Next, biologists trained the condors to fear humans so they would avoid human settlements, where they were likely to get into trouble. To instill fear of humans, keepers at the Los Angeles Zoo would sneak up behind a condor. Then they would pick it up and turn it on its back. (Condors apparently hate being turned upside down!) With such conditioning, more condors have been released into the wild, at three different sites in California. Since the training began, none of the condors has been injured on power poles. As of February 1996, seventeen condors were in the wild in California. Six California condors were released in Arizona on December 12, 1996.

CALIFORNIA CONDOR
Gymnogyps californianus

ORDER: Falconiformes
FAMILY: Carthartridae
GENUS: *Gymnogyps*
SPECIES: *californianus*

Working with sandhill cranes, scientists first got the birds to imprint on humans in sandhill costumes.

Next the birds imprinted on an ultralight plane.

Then the birds followed the aircraft from Idaho to New Mexico.

Currently, efforts to save whooping cranes are continuing. The birds are being raised in captivity and introduced into the wild. The habitat areas in Texas are managed so that food is plentiful for the cranes. The major threat to the cranes' survival is collision with power lines during their migration. The gradual destruction of their major wintering site, the Aransas National Wildlife Refuge, is a problem, too. In the 1940s, the Gulf Intracoastal Waterway was dug right where the whooping cranes live. The boat traffic on this canal has disturbed the nearby marshes, and the soil in the marsh is slowly eroding. Chemical contamination, from boat fuel and from cargo carried by barges is also a concern.

Biologists continue their extraordinary efforts to save the whooping cranes. As of 1996, 225 whooping cranes were living in the wild, and 131 in captivity. Recent successes breeding cranes and introducing them into the wild give biologists hope this bird species can be saved. Scientists are also using what they have learned with whooping cranes to save rare crane species in other parts of the world. Programs to breed cranes, protect habitat, restore habitat, and reintroduce captive cranes into the wild are being carried out in Vietnam, Myanmar, China, Mongolia, Afghanistan, India, Pakistan, Iran, and other countries.

WHAT DOES THE FUTURE
HOLD FOR ENDANGERED BIRDS?

Every year, in late December and again in May, more than forty thousand members of the National Audubon Society spend all day counting birds. They walk sidewalks, hike trails, drive roads, wander wetlands, and peer at bird feeders in backyards. These bird counts are the society's best attempt at figuring out just how many birds of each species there are. During summer, birders also count nests and hatching birds in a survey of breeding birds.

What bird counters have been finding, and what birders have known for a while, is that many birds that were once plentiful have become scarce. Of particular concern are Neotropical migrants—birds that migrate from Mexico, Central America, South America, and the Caribbean, into the United States and Canada. Almost one-half of the birds that nest in North America are Neotropical migrants. These birds include warblers, orioles, tanagers, and other birdwatchers' favorites. Radar studies of the number of birds migrating over the Gulf of Mexico show that spring migrants have decreased by about 50 percent in the last thirty years.

Part of this decrease is probably due to the destruction of tropical forests. But a significant share of the problem occurs on the migrants' breeding grounds in the United States and Canada. Many warblers, thrushes, and other birds need large areas of forest to nest and raise young. Forests fragmented by timber cutting, developments, and roads do not make good habitat for these birds. Nest parasites such as cowbirds, and nest predators such as raccoons and domestic cats, prowl the edges of roads, clearings, and fields. Both nest parasites and nest predators decrease the number of young warblers, tanagers, and gnatcatchers that are raised. Birds passing close to buildings often collide with windows and die.

Forest birds are not the only ones decreasing in number. The populations of grassland birds such as grasshopper sparrows have also decreased drastically. Birds that depend on riparian habitat—riverside trees, shrubs, and plants—are also at great risk. Along coastlines, shorebirds and water birds are threatened by persistent, daily pollution from factories, sewage, and runoff, as well as dramatic pollution incidents—oil spills such as the *Exxon Valdez* oil spill in Alaska in 1989.

• HAWAIIAN BIRDS AND EXOTIC PROBLEMS •

The Hawaiian islands contain only two-tenths of 1 percent of the land area in the United States. Yet twenty-eight of the ninety birds listed as endangered or threatened in the United States live only in Hawaii. Among these birds are the endangered néne, also called the Hawaiian goose; the endangered io, also called the Hawaiian hawk; the alala, also called the Hawaiian crow; plus many colorful finches and honeycreepers.

Néne, or Hawaiian goose

The overall decline of bird populations is an important part of the issue of endangered species. More and more, conservationists are turning their attention not just to saving the rarest birds, but also to preserving the common ones. Preventing the problems that face these birds may be much easier than restoring a population later, because last-ditch attempts to save birds through captive breeding efforts can be difficult and extremely expensive.

SPECIES SAVED   Twenty-five years ago, bald eagles—the symbol of the United States—had almost disappeared from many states. But today,

---

Hawaii changed radically when human settlers arrived from Polynesia about 1,500 years ago. They cleared the land for growing bananas, breadfruit, taro, and sugarcane. Hunters killed off the island's twenty species of flightless birds. The large birds were easy to hunt and good to eat. Settlers from Polynesia, and later Europe, brought animals and plants from their homes. They brought pigs, chickens, dogs, goats, and cats. Other animals—rats, ants, and the like—stowed away on ships in crates of imported goods. Soon, Hawaii's plants and animals were competing with animals from all over the world.

Today, Hawaii is a changed place. The green plants and colorful flowers you see on much of the island are imported plants that have escaped and now grow wild. Most native species of animals and plants survive on remote islands or atop steep mountains, where exotic species have not yet reached. Some of these areas are protected in national parks, but even there, native animals and plants are in danger. The biggest problem is exotic, or nonnative animals such as goats, mongooses, and rats. More than one hundred thousand feral pigs roam the islands, digging up plants, destroying birds' nests, and generally wreaking havoc on the forest.

Since people settled the Hawaiian Islands, an estimated half of the native birds have become extinct. In the last 220 years, seventeen species and six subspecies have died out. Conservationists are working on saving the remaining birds through many different programs throughout the islands. Chief among these efforts is habitat preservation and removal of pigs, goats, and rats from parks. An ambitious program of captive breeding is also helping keep endangered birds such as the néne alive.

bald eagles are back, and thriving. The birds are doing so well that the U.S. Fish and Wildlife Service has changed their status from "endangered" to "threatened" in the lower forty-eight United States. (Bald eagles were never rare in Alaska and do not live in Hawaii.)

In the 1960s, scientists noticed the eggs of bald eagles, brown pelicans, and peregrine falcons had unusually thin shells. The eggs were being crushed by the weight of the adult birds incubating the eggs. In the late 1960s, scientists recognized the link between thin eggshells and pesticides in the environment. The pesticide DDT was being sprayed on wetlands, and even on housing developments in order to kill mosquitoes. The runoff from the land and the pesticide sprayed directly into wetlands, ended up in lakes and streams. The pesticide built up in fish, and fish-eating birds such as falcons, eagles, and pelicans accumulated high concentrations of pesticides in their bodies. The DDT interfered with the proper formation of eggs.

To combat the problem, in 1972, DDT was banned in the United States. After DDT was banned, no one knew if the eagle, falcon, and pelican populations would ever recover. But they did. Banning the pesticide was a major factor in the recovery. Additional help for eagles and falcons came from the Endangered Species Act of 1973. Once bald eagles were declared a threatened species, and peregrine falcons were declared endangered, under that law, their nesting habitats were protected. Poisoning or shooting bald eagles and peregrine falcons became illegal. Captive breeding and the release of bald eagles and peregrine falcons into the wild also helped to reestablish these birds in areas where they had died out.

Today the birds are doing so well that the U.S. Fish and Wildlife Service is planning to change the status of peregrine falcons from endangered to threatened. Peregrine falcons are even being released in cities, where they nest on skyscrapers and hunt pigeons to eat! The brown pelican, too, has rebounded, expanding its range even more than was expected.

Pesticides, however, are still a major threat to the health of birds and other animals, including people. Eagles near the Great Lakes are being born with life-threatening deformities such as twisted beaks. Levels of PCBs, another poisonous substance, are high in fish-eating birds near the Great Lakes. And unfortunately, DDT and other harmful pesticides outlawed in the United States are still being manufactured by U.S. companies and exported for use in Mexico, Central America, South America, and the

*T*he pesticide DDT has been linked to thin eggshells in brown pelicans and other birds.

Caribbean. Action still needs to be taken to solve the pesticide problem. But past successes give people hope that the job can be done.

WHAT'S BEING DONE TO SAVE BIRDS

Most of today's bird conservation efforts focus on preserving habitat. After all, providing an animal with habitat is the best, long-term way to ensure its survival. The previous chapters have mentioned many of the programs run by government agencies, conservation groups, and private citizens to save endangered birds. Here's a small sampling of numerous other efforts hoping to accomplish the same thing:

- In the United States, Canada, and Mexico, people are turning their own backyards and schoolyards into better bird habitats, by putting up nesting boxes, planting trees, shrubs, and flowers, and providing water, as well. Not only do these changes benefit birds, they benefit the people, who also get closeup views of more birds. The National Wildlife Federation has officially certified thousands of these backyard and schoolyard habitats, through their Backyard Habitat Program.

Thousands of backyards like this one have been certified as official Backyard Habitats by the National Wildlife Federation.

- Through Birder's Exchange, birdwatchers can donate binoculars, tripods, cameras, sleeping bags, books, field guides, computers, and other equipment—new or used, but in good condition. This equipment is distributed to needy scientists, researchers, naturalists, park rangers, educators, and young naturalists in twenty-two countries in Latin America and in the Caribbean.

- RARE Center for Tropical Conservation is helping increase environmental awareness in countries throughout the Caribbean and parts of Central America by building people's national pride in native birds and in other animals. Although the organization is based in Philadelphia, only six people work there. Its main organizers are people local to each country. In Belize, Rafael Manzanero travels to hundreds of schools, teaching children about the keel-billed toucan, now Belize's national bird. His efforts are encouraging kids to stop killing the birds with slingshots, and adults to preserve the habitat toucans need. Efforts in other countries have focused on rare birds and butterflies.

School children in Belize are learning to recognize and appreciate the keel-billed toucan, their national bird.

- Some farmers are helping with bird conservation. They are working to reduce the use of harmful pesticides by rotating crops and by using other conservation techniques. Hay farmers are timing the mowing of fields so birds have a chance to nest and raise their young before the tractors come through. In California, farmers are flooding their fields after their autumn harvests. Migrating birds stop at these spots, feeding on what is leftover from crops grown in the fields.

- Through a network of public and private organizations called Partners in Flight, people all over North America, South America, Central America, and the Caribbean, are doing research, and exchanging information about migrating birds and habitat conservation. Birds tend to migrate along well-established routes, skirting coastlines and funneling through certain areas. Habitats in these areas are particularly important to millions of migrating birds that rest and feed at these spots along their journeys, which may be thousands of miles long.

Through Partners in Flight, grants have been given to purchase and protect rain forest in Costa Rica, to study better management of grasslands and forests, to study toxins in loons, and other worthwhile projects.

It is truly mind boggling how many people in North America are working to help endangered birds and how many creative programs are in progress. To find out how you can get involved in bird conservation efforts, consult the "How You Can Help Birds" section near the end of this book.

LESSONS LEARNED AND FUTURE PLANS

In the years since the Endangered Species Act was passed, some efforts to save bird populations have been successful and some have failed. Along the way, government officials, conservationists, and scientists have learned lessons that may help them in the future.

One important lesson is that every bird, and every habitat, is different and needs its own kind of management. What works in one area may not work in another. Not all forests are alike. For instance, cutting the trees and burning the land would be disastrous for the threatened spotted owls in the Pacific Northwest. But for Kirtland's warblers, who live in jack pine forests, this type of forest management helps them survive.

Another lesson is that ensuring the health of birds and their habitats often means managing lands in ways that mimic natural cycles. In the Everglades, scientists are reengineering water systems to match natural cycles of floods and droughts. In South Carolina, to help red-cockaded woodpeckers, biologists must set fires, like the natural, lightning-set ones, so pine trees will reproduce.

Conservationists have also realized that getting people who live locally to support conservation efforts can make those programs go more smoothly. Encouraging people to take pride in endangered species and showing them how they can benefit indirectly from endangered species can help conservation succeed. Residents near the Kirtland's warbler preserve in Michigan benefit from the related tourism—people come to see the birds and bring revenue to the community.

What people have learned about endangered species in the last few decades is leading them to a whole new vision for the future. Many endangered species experts want to move away from saving species one by one.

They believe it would be better to look at the big picture, preserving large chunks of unique ecosystems, instead. Preserving an ecosystem and keeping it healthy would, of course, save the species that live there.

For now, the Endangered Species Act is the best legislation available to save ecosystems. When spotted owls are preserved, their old growth forests homes are, too. But in the future, many people hope legislators will recognize the issue is not just saving a few owls, but also preserving a unique and complex ecosystem.

HOW YOU CAN HELP BIRDS

Here are some suggestions for things you can do to help endangered birds and bird populations in general:

- Learn more about endangered birds and environmental issues by contacting some of the following organizations:

American Birding Association, P.O. Box 6599, Colorado Springs, CO 80934; phone 1-800-850-2473. Information on birding in North America.

Center for Environmental Information, 50 West Main Street, Rochester, NY 14614; phone 1-716-262-2870. Provides environmental information.

Committee on the Status of Endangered Wildlife in Canada (COSEWIC), Renew Secretariat, c/o Canadian Wildlife Service, Environment Canada, Ottawa, ONT K1A OH3; phone 1-613-997-4991. Provides teacher materials and status reports on specific endangered birds.

Cornell Laboratory of Ornithology, 159 Sapsucker Woods Road, Ithaca, NY 14850; phone 1-607-254-2473. Publishes a catalog of bird-related products, and *Wild Bird* magazine. Runs a bird feeder survey.

International Crane Foundation, E-11376 Shady Lane Road, Baraboo, WI 53913-9778. Provides fact sheets about cranes.

National Audubon Society, 700 Broadway, New York, NY 10003-9562; phone 1-212-979-3000. Provides information on endangered birds and environmental issues related to conservation.

National Wildlife Federation, 1400 16th Street N.W., Washington, DC 20036-2266; phone 1-202-797-6800. Provides information on endangered species and how to improve backyard/schoolyard habitat for wild birds.

The Nature Conservancy, 1815 North Lynn Street, Arlington, VA 22209; phone 1-703-841-5300. This organization buys and protects land, much of which provides habitats for endangered species.

The Peregrine Fund, 566 West Flying Hawk Lane, Boise, Idaho 83709; phone 1-208-362-8687. Provides information on peregrine falcons and many other endangered birds.

U.S. Fish and Wildlife Service, Office of Publications, 1849 C Street N.W., Webb Building, MS 130, Washington, DC 20240; phone 1-703-358-1711. They provide a list of endangered species. They also publish the *Endangered Species Technical Bulletin,* the major source of information on government programs to save endangered species. You may be able to find it in libraries, often as part of *The Endangered Species Update.*

World Wildlife Fund, 1250 24th Street N.W., Suite 400, Washington, DC 20037; phone 1-202-293-4800. Provides information on endangered species, particularly illegal trade in wildlife products. Has educational materials on biodiversity.

World Wildlife Fund Canada, 90 Eglinton Avenue East, Suite 504, Toronto, ONT M45 2Z7; phone 1-416-489-8800. Provides information on endangered species in Canada.

- The *Citizen's Guide to Migratory Bird Conservation* has the most comprehensive, up-to-date information on how you can help migratory birds and birds in general. To obtain a copy, send $5.00 for one copy, or $2.00 each for five or more copies, to the Cornell Lab of Ornithology. Make checks payable to the Cornell Lab of Ornithology. Send them to the address listed on page 84. The booklet gives background on the threats to migratory birds, tips on how to help birds, and addresses to contact for more information. Once you have the book, take some of the actions it suggests!

- Attract birds to your backyard, schoolyard, or local park by improving the habitat for birds. You can plant trees and shrubs that provide berries and nectar that birds eat and branches where they can nest. Put up bird feeders. Install a wildlife pond or birdbath where birds can obtain water. Do plenty of research first, to find out what plants are good for birds and grow well in your part of the country. And be sure to get the permission and help of parents, guardians, teachers, park rangers, and property owners! For information on how to improve habitat for wildlife, check your local library for books. You can also contact the National Wildlife Federation about their backyard habitat program. See page 84 for the address.

- Collect good-quality, new, or used equipment and donate it to the Birder's Exchange. Ask your parents, guardians, or other family members, and friends whether they have equipment they are not using that they could donate. You could get your class, scout troop, or other local group involved in the effort. The Birder's Exchange will distribute these items to bird conservation programs in Latin American and Caribbean countries. Binoculars, spotting scopes, cameras, lenses, tents, backpacks, field guides, and other equipment are all needed. For information, contact:

Birder's Exchange
Manomet Observatory
P.O. Box 1770
81 Stage Point Road
Manomet, MA 02345
Phone 1-508-224-6521
Fax 1-508-224-9220

- Volunteer for the birds. Contact nearby parks, nature centers, and local Audubon Society chapters to find out what volunteer efforts you can join. You may be able to count birds, check nests, fill bird feeders, plant bird-attracting plants, help run an education program, make posters, build birdhouses, put up bluebird boxes, make phone calls . . . the possibilities abound!

- Educate others about birds and bird conservation. Write an article or letter to the editor for your local paper or school paper. Put up posters. Give a talk. Write a play. Put together a video or a spot for a local radio station. Or come up with your own creative publicity ideas!

- Keep domestic cats indoors and away from bird feeders and nesting sites. This is especially important in spring and early summer when chicks are learning to fly and cannot easily escape from cats.

- If you find an injured bird, contact a local wildlife rehabilitation center, nature center, museum, or Audubon Society. Someone there should be able to put you in touch with a licensed wildlife rehabilitator. It is illegal to capture and care for wild birds without a special license.

- Turn off lights, televisions, and other appliances when you are not using them. Reduce unnecessary car trips by walking, bicycling, taking buses, or combining trips. Saving oil, gas, and electricity reduces the need for oil drilling and transport, which leads to oil spills that pollute areas where birds live. Encourage your family to use energy-saving devices in your home. For energy-saving tips, contact your local electric utility. For a catalog of energy-saving appliances, write or call:

Real Goods
966 Mazzoni Street
Ukiah, CA 95482-3471
Phone 1-800-762-7325

- Use paper and wood products wisely and sparingly. Recycle newspapers and white paper whenever possible. This helps reduce the need for cutting trees from forests where birds live. For recycled paper products, check at local stores. You can also order recycled paper and environmental products from:

Seventh Generation
Colchester, Vermont 05446-1672
Phone 1-800-456-1177

- Write letters to elected officials, telling them your concerns about endangered birds. To write to your congress members, use the following addresses:

The Honorable (insert the name of your representative)
U.S. House of Representatives
Washington, DC 20515

The Honorable (insert the name of your senator)
U.S. Senate
Washington, DC 20510

GLOSSARY

artificial insemination   a technique used with captive animals that are not mating successfully. The female animal is injected with sperm from the male animal to fertilize the female's eggs.

brood parasite   a bird, such as cowbird, that sneaks its own egg into other bird species' nests, so the host bird spends its time and energy raising the "adopted" bird instead of its own. (In this way, a brood parasite interferes with another bird's raising of its young, called its brood.)

DDT   an abbreviation for dichloro-diphenyl-trichloro-ethane, an insecticide used widely, especially for mosquito control, until it was banned in 1972 in the United States. It is still used in other countries.

endangered species   species that are in danger of becoming extinct

exotic species   species that are not native to a particular area

extinct species   species that have died out

generalist   a species that can eat many different kinds of foods and tolerate a wide range of environmental conditions. Generalists often live in several different habitats.

genetic diversity   the variety of different genes present in the individuals of a population

home range   the area an animal roams and uses in its daily activities

imprinting   the learning process by which a newborn animal recognizes and bonds with another animal that it considers its parent

inbreeding   the mating of closely related organisms. Inbreeding can increase the frequency of inherited defects.

population   a group of organisms of the same species that inhabits a specific area

prescribed burn   controlled fires that are set on purpose by land managers to restore a habitat

raptor   a bird of prey such as a hawk. Raptors have strong talons for catching prey.

rookery a site where birds gather in large numbers to nest

specialist an organism that eats a narrow range of foods and/or has very specific habitat needs

species a group of genetically similar organisms that tend to breed together and produce fertile offspring under natural conditions

subspecies a population of organisms isolated from others of their species, so that they only breed with members of their population. If they remain isolated, a subspecies may eventually evolve distinctive characteristics and become a separate species.

succession the process by which one natural community of organisms gradually replaces another

threatened species a species that is declining in number and is plagued by such serious problems that it is likely to become endangered

FOR FURTHER INFORMATION

Books:

(Books geared especially for young people are noted with an asterisk.)

*Banks, Martin. *Endangered Wildlife*. Vero Beach, Fla.: Rourke Enterprises, 1988.

Braus, Judy, editor. *Endangered Species: Wild & Rare*. Washington, DC: National Wildlife Federation, 1989.

DiSilvestro, Roger L. *The Endangered Kingdom: The Struggle to Save America's Wildlife*. New York: John Wiley & Sons, 1989.

Ehrlich, Paul R., David S. Dobkin, and Darryle Wheye. *Birds in Jeopardy: The Imperiled and Extinct Birds of the United States and Canada, Including Hawaii and Puerto Rico*. Stanford: Stanford University Press, 1992.

Elphick, Jonathan, editor. *The Atlas of Bird Migration*. New York: Random House, 1995.

Emanoil, Mary, editor. *Encyclopedia of Endangered Species*. Detroit: Gale Research, 1994.

Halpin, Anne, and The National Wildlife Federation. *For the Birds!: A Handy Guide to Attracting Birds to Your Backyard*. New York: Holt, 1996.

*Javna, John. *50 Simple Things Kids Can Do to Save the Earth*. Kansas City: Andrews and McMeel, 1990.

Katz, Barbara. *So Cranes May Dance: A Rescue from the Brink of Extinction*. Chicago: Chicago Review Press, 1993.

Kaufman, Kenn. *Lives of North American Birds*. Boston: Houghton Mifflin, 1996.

*Lasky, Kathryn. *She's Wearing a Dead Bird on Her Head!* New York: Hyperion, 1995.

McFarlane, Robert W. *A Stillness in the Pines, the Ecology of the Red-Cockaded Woodpecker*. New York: W. W. Norton & Company, 1992.

Matthews, John R., and Charles J. Moseley, editors. *The Official World Wildlife Fund Guide to Endangered Species of North America*. Washington, DC: Beacham, 1990.

*Nilson, Greta. *The Endangered Species Handbook*. Washington, DC: The Animal Welfare Institute, 1986.

Schreiber, R. L., A. W. Diamond, R. T. Peterson, and W. Cronkite. *Save the Birds*. Boston: Houghton Mifflin, 1989.

*Silverstein, Alvin, et. al. *The Peregrine Falcon*. Brookfield, Conn.: Millbrook, 1995.

Terborgh, John. *Where Have All the Birds Gone?* Princeton, N.J.: Princeton University Press, 1989.

MAGAZINES:

Check your local library, newsstand, or bookstore for these magazines, which frequently feature articles on endangered birds:

Audubon, National Audubon Society, 700 Broadway, New York, NY 10003-9501; phone 1-212-979-3000.
Birder's World, Subscription Information, P.O. Box 52700, Boulder, CO 80322-2700; phone 1-800-753-4873.
Birding, American Birding Association, P.O. Box 6599, Colorado Springs, CO 80934; phone 1-800-634-7736.
Birdwatcher's Digest, P.O. Box 110, Marietta, Ohio 45750; phone 1-800-879-2473.

SELECTED ARTICLES ABOUT ENDANGERED BIRDS

AUDUBON:

Chadwick, Douglas. "Strength in Humility," January–February 1996, 46–47.
Graham, Frank, Jr. "Kite *vs.* Stork," May 1990, 104–110.
Line, Les. "Massachusetts Miracle: Piping Plovers Return to New England," March–April 1996, 20–24.
Middleton, Susan, and David Liittchwager. "Parting Shots? Formal Portraits of Species on the Brink," January–February, 1996, 40–45.
Williams, Ted. "Finding Safe Harbor," January–February 1996, 26–32.

NATIONAL GEOGRAPHIC:

Balog, James. "A Personal Vision of Vanishing Wildlife," April 1990, 84–103.
Chadwick, Douglas. "Dead or Alive: The Endangered Species Act," March 1995, 2–41.
Duplaix, Nicole. "South Florida Water: Paying the Price," July 1990, 89–113.
Royte, Elizabeth. "On the Brink: Hawaii's Vanishing Species," September 1995, 2–37.

INTERNATIONAL WILDLIFE:

Turbak, Gary. "A Reason to Whoop," January–February 1990, 12–16.

US NEWS AND WORLD REPORT:

Carpenter, Betsy. "Back from the Abyss: Scientists Might Save the California Condor. But Is It Worth the Price?" October 14, 1991, 63–64.

COMPUTER-BASED INFORMATION SOURCES:

The U.S. Fish and Wildlife Service, the government agency that oversees the endangered species program, can be reached through a home computer on the World Wide Web. Their home page address is **http://www.fws.gov/**

Their home page contains the updated list of endangered and threatened species, state lists of endangered species, the text of *The Endangered Species Bulletin*, and other information.

If you do not have access to the World Wide Web, you can reach them on the Internet by e-mail at **R9IRMLIB@FWS.gov**

When you e-mail them, type: {**Send ES Instructions**} on the subject line, and they will send you a list of the retrieval commands for information available.

INDEX

References to illustrations are listed in *italic, **boldface*** type.

ABOUT THE AUTHOR

April Pulley Sayre is the author of seventeen natural history books for young readers, including a book about field scientists called *Put on Some Antlers and Walk Like a Moose*. Her picture book, *If You Should Hear a Honey Guide*, received a pointer review in Kirkus and was called "the outstanding children's natural history title for 1995," by *Smithsonian* magazine. The first three volumes in Sayre's twelve-book, "Exploring Earth's Biomes" series for middle school readers received starred reviews in *Booklist*. Her articles have appeared in *World, Ranger Rick*, and the *Earth Explorer Encyclopedia* (CD-ROM). She also produces science videos.

Sayre is known for diving into her subjects. She and her husband wade through wetlands, hike through deserts, camp in tropical rain forests, and snorkel over coral reefs while pursuing their personal and professional interest in wildlife and the environment. They recently coauthored a book about hummingbirds. Although Sayre writes on a wide range of topics, among her specialties are endangered species, offbeat animals, and birds of any kind. Originally from Greenville, South Carolina, she now lives in South Bend, Indiana— in between adventures.